T0113412

A HARLEM MOON CLASSIC

OTHER HARLEM MOON CLASSICS

Pride of Family: Four Generations of American Women of Color by Carole Ione

The Quest of the Silver Fleece by W.E.B. Du Bois

SOULSCRIPT

*

A Collection of
African American Poetry

Edited by
JUNE JORDAN

HARLEM MOON

Broadway Books

New York

Contents

___

SAYING THE PERSON

ATTITUDES OF SOUL

Foreword

STACEYANN CHIN

In an age before teen pop-star cyber-journals became more widely read than poetry anthologies, June Jordan, in the summer of her too-brief tenure with us, understood that the collective voice of the voiceless is still one of the most powerful tools of change. The tradition of outlining brown bodies, brown stories, each with its own experience and particular inclination of telling, is bravely inked onto the pages of *soulscript.*

The poems here acknowledge a world careening out of control, a spinning that, for faces of the Diaspora, began before we needed to mark our skins with black, or Latino, or Caribbean, or immigrant. And yet, amidst the tearing and screaming, hope lingers between the black and white lines, between the grandeur of what we long for and the squalor that presses cruel against the heels of the surviving spirit.

June Jordan, the visionary, the poet, the editor of this important milestone in the etching of the blueprint toward a kinder future, believed there was room enough in publishing for every voice that found itself speaking. She took every opportunity to remind us that, in our silence, we participate in every horror perpetrated against the oppressed on the planet. In her essay "Do You Do Well to Be Angry," published in the collection *Some of Us Did Not Die* (Basic *Civitas* Books, 2003) she invites us each to admit:

Sometimes, I am the terrorist I must disarm.

I first read those words in February of 2004; twenty months after June had crossed over, seven months before the third anniversary of the collapse of the World Trade Center, and two days into my second visit, in as many months, to the continent of Australia. My hotel room in Melbourne was quaint: white sheets, large windows, Sony microwave, and the Panasonic evening news—alight with the excitement of a riot in the Aboriginal "ghetto community of Redfern."

In a breathless rush, the reporter describes the police, the teargas, the bullets used to subdue the residents. Not to worry, though, everything was under control and the white chief of police (with the thick British accent) would be on spot in a few minutes to assure us we were safe from such "evil acts of terrorism."

Three years after September 11, 2001, the allegations and explanations were still a wet muddle of half-truths and conspiracy theories gone wild. I had just, months before, left the Broadway cast of Russell Simmons's *Def Poetry Jam.* I lacked direction. My fingers were still quiet from the year I had spent becoming thirty, dealing with the massive changes in my body, my career, my relationship with Jamaica, and the fact that I had yet to do anything with the almost three hundred pages of a memoir I had been nursing for at least four years by then.

Alone and silently clawing at myself, for not sleeping enough, not eating enough, and not writing enough, I mourned the buildings and the bodies that had perished there. To make sense of my own tacit list-lessness, I decided to read what June had written of it. And *wham!* Broad as daylight—there, sat the ultimate challenge. I had to rewind and read it again.

Sometimes, I am the terrorist I must disarm.

The brutal truth of her position was so clear I began the permanent shift that would reconfigure the way I saw the use of the word as polit-ical tool. I was no longer simply lesbian, or Jamaican, or woman. I was now, like June, writing as a Palestinian, as a Native American, a Zulu in South Africa; I was now writing to indict myself in the war against the powerless. The initial draft of a bleeding *First Letter to the remaining Aborigines in Australia* was the result of a transformation that was even more heightened when I noted that the strange absence of Native American faces in North America was congruent to the erasure of the Aboriginal flesh from the visible landscape of Australia.

Soon after, Harlem Moon editor Clarence A. Haynes called to invite me to write the foreword for an anthology that June Jordan had edited. I kept thinking that June's entire life was about making the dialogue around human rights more inclusive of the invisible, that I wanted to be more like that in my own charting of tales and telling. As I read poem after poem, it seemed fitting to present, as part of the foreword, the very poem, jolted from me by the phrase written by June Jordan, that had left me so wounded. Immediately after reading *soulscript,* I finished the construct that may well become the philosophical corner-stone upon which I should hang all subsequent poems pulled from my fingers.

My whole life
National Geographic has sold your tribal markings
as the fashion of Down Under

and yet
after two days sunning under the Sydney sky I have seen
no trace of your decorated faces
only the backs of these shadows sleeping drunk
on the city's sidewalks
*   not so much beggars as*
people prevented from choosing
their own destiny
*   not alone in the global community*
the Seminoles
reflect your predicament in Florida
*   Zulus prance their image on silver coins*
for tourism in South Africa
*   not one Arawak remains in the mirror of my Xamaica*
. . . there are rumors of your numbers
disappearing into the dark of Hyde Park
the well-kept grounds just left of
Liverpool
north of Elizabeth Street
modern reality smeared
with the stains of the Old Empire
*   the educated in New Delhi still speak*
*   English with a British accent*
*   it is no accident that Blair and Bush*
have buried the trans-Atlantic hatchet
to pool resources
in response to the emerging head of a United States of Europe

June's political poetry collided with my love of words a mere few months into my own journey towards writing a Jamaican, lesbian, Asian, living-in-America self into a contemporary history. June had the ability relevantly to include causes that seemed to have nothing to do with her personal suffering. It made sense that she would claim her Blackness as Palestinian-ness as Queerness. Her essays and poems encouraged me to join the rant for Nicaragua, the lament for Afghanistan, Lebanon, South Africa, and India—no place seemed too remote or unconnected to the fate of the world we should all be writing to create.

Poetry as I have come to know it is aware of what is happening in the "now." It connects the repetition of atrocities with the healing nature of time. It reduces the terror of the cosmic to the rapture of the microscopic. Everything affects everything else. The direction of my gaze today is the direction of the rally of tomorrow.

All eyes are on the East
new age Napoleons poised toward possession
   —savage intentions
make hidden weapons of teenagers in Qatar

the poor in Tehran watch helpless
as CNN reports the blood-wet deaths of ordinary
Israelis kneeling for prayer in Tel Aviv
the collective heart of the West
hardens against Palestinians clawing
body parts from the rubble of Arafat's last
argument with Sharon

Nothing interrupts the boyish
bickering—the blatant bartering of one life
for another
   —soldiers/refugees
victims of the indifferent hands carving artificial borders
across lands that had no boundaries before we got there

Here is to the pens that have always known
we are our brother's keeper

Responsibility washes all our hands
with the guilt of association
if there is to be peace with compassion
it must begin with the me

Sometimes I am the terrorist I must disarm

we—each must find the restraint
to curb the ego of our own consumption
each well-fed body must stand trial
for crimes of poverty and violence against the other
each invisible face
must be found and accounted for
the Untouchable
the leper
the woman
the orphan
the Cuban
the faggot
the face
pushed to the edge of existence

I am the Jamaican
hunting for signs of the Aboriginal in Australia

show me you are still connected to all this land
show yourselves as magic or moonlight
or master plan

an ordinary band of bodies
rising up strange among these buildings like blades of grass
break open the tinted windows
rewrite your true history on the new
transparent glass

Gwendolyn Brooks, Naomi Long Madgett, Nikki Giovanni, Audre Lorde, Sonia Sanchez, Claude McKay, and June Jordan are only a few of the veteran activists who have written about their fathers and daughters, written tributes to other activists, and written about the state of our lives in the face of the "global creep." Younger voices have also been introduced. The circle of life is in full breath here. Courage and commitment to difficult truths, the sense of urgency and importance of knowing which stories, both personal and cultural, have shaped the human struggle, are all embedded in these pages. Olympus, Kilimanjaro, Chicago, New York, Vietnam, Malcolm X, Ray Charles—the list of places and people referenced and dealt with is endless.

Soulscript is a toast to all the poems, novels, and essays that have stirred us toward action. It is a challenge to those of us left holding the torch of change, an invocation to disarm our own narrow agendas; it is a mandate for all those living to put pen to paper and march the masses toward a more meaningful collage of the self.

Introduction

———

(*originally published in 1970*)

C oast to coast, on subways, in bedrooms, in kitchens, in weekend
workshops, at parties—almost anywhere except the classroom,
as a matter of fact—Afro-Americans are writing poetry. It's happening
now, and it's wonderful, fine, and limitless, like love—that love the sis-
ters and the brothers exchange inside the family living here. And when
American classrooms switch from confrontation to communion, black
poetry will happen in the schools as well.

Poetry tells the feeling.

A poem tells relationship.

By picturing a street for freedom, or by rhyming *whitestare* with
nightmare, or by laying down lines the way a man runs crazy, poetry re-
veals the various feelings of relationship. People live a poem every
minute they spend in the world. Reaction, memory, and dream: these

are the springs of poetry. And a four-year-old flows among them as fully as any adult.

Since poetry turns the individual drama of being human into words, it is an art open to all vocabulary made personal. Poetry changes life into a written drama where words set the stage and where words then act as the characters on that stage.

Soulscript presents the poetry of Afro-Americans.

Over the past several years, Afro-America has flourished as a national community concerned to express its own situation and its own response. The concern to choose, find, and create relationship leads naturally into poems. Here, in this anthology, the reader will follow along where Afro-American concern for a vocabulary-made-personal leads. Governed by a beautiful, proud spirit, the Afro-American grows from the experience of brave, continuing survival despite the force of deadly circumstance. These poems tell that spirit and that survival, even as they spell black dreams.

Language is something common, something always shared—like air. The human voice depends on air. Poetry depends on language. But voice transforms the air into a spoken personality. And poetry transforms a language into voice. Poems are voiceprints of language, or if you prefer, *soulscript*. In part, the problems of poetry-writing stem from the nature of its material: language as everybody's identical tool.

The craft of poetry is an everlasting challenge to the language blur of individuality.

This struggle to determine and then preserve a particular, human voice is closely related to the historic struggling of black life in America.

Slavery meant that certain men comfortably destroyed other, real people as individuals. Enslaved, black men and women were forced into the status merely of machines making money for the "master." Literally lashed into a role rejecting particular, human life, the cultivation of *own voice* became a workaday occupation, an unrelenting protest, and an ultimate social triumph. After slavery, the Afro-American fought to stay alive in a land amused by stereotypes hostile to the integrity of his person.

Just as Malcolm Little redefined his self into Malcolm X, Afro-America, for its integrity and survival, pursues this history into pride and poem. We must redefine the words, the names, of our universe and the values attached to every written tag—such as *white, black, darkness, light, good,* and *evil.* And indeed, from San Francisco to Brooklyn, from Watts to Fort Greene, we are working into poetry the future of our love.

In all forms of personally crafted language, there is an exceptional, lengthy tradition of black American literature. From the time of Frederick Douglass down through Eldridge Cleaver, Afro-American leaders of first rank have been distinguished by extraordinary, unique word-power. If we will remember the relations between poetry and language, there is scarcely reason for surprise at the wealth of outstanding poets among black people. Even less surprising is the frequency of black political figures who are also poets. For example: Julian Bond, LeRoi Jones, Julius Lester. And yet, the youngest reader may be shocked to consider that, until quite recently, most black literature remained unpublished. This neglect was hardly accidental. Literature, the crafting of language by special, human experience, acts as a witness. Great literature acts as an unforgettable, completely convincing witness. Poetry raises the human voice from the flat, familiar symbols on a paper page. Great poetry compels an answering; the raised voice creates communion. Until recently, the Afro-American witness suffered an alien censorship. And even as slaves were not allowed to congregate alone, to create communion of their own, poetry has been recognized as dangerous by the enemies of free men everywhere. Consequently, the typical textbook offers the poetry of Carl Sandburg, Hart Crane, Amy Lowell, and e. e. cummings (white American poets), protected from competition from Jean Toomer, Margaret Walker, Countee Cullen, and Robert Hayden.

(Who?)

However, the weight of alien censorship is lifting. James Weldon Johnson's line "O Black and Unknown Bards" no longer predicts the public career of written Black Art.

Yet the weight lifts slowly, and as it does, still another barrier to normal recognition meets the Afro-American. A discouraging number of published critics pretend that the literature, the poetry, of black artists buckles like some inferior stuff when measured by the usual criteria. This is a patronizing, absolute mistake. To be consistent, such critics would have to deny the artistic validity of world literature characterized by social conscience and the perilous heroism of rebellion. W. B. Yeats, Stephen Vincent Benét, and Federico García Lorca are simply a few whose political commitment would compromise the admiration they now command as poets.

In *soulscript*, the poetry of Afro-America appears as it was written: in tears, in rage, in hope, in sonnet, in blank/free verse, in overwhelming rhetorical scream. These poems redeem a hostile vocabulary; they witness, they create communion, and they contribute beauty to the long evening of their origins.

To emphasize the living purpose of black poetry, I have chosen the poems primarily of people who could read them aloud next week. Privileged as the editor, my difficulty has been to delimit rather than to secure. Given the time and volume, these poems would appear as the fractional part of an entire literature that they really are. More than one poet, for instance Jay Wright and Calvin Hernton, would have much heavier representation but distance, changing address, and like complications have prevented the inclusion of many poems here. *Soulscript* opens with the poetry written by black children ranging in age from twelve to eighteen. These young poets, more or less accidentally known by me, should powerfully suggest the fabulous efflorescence of black literary art that we, Afro-American and white, can enjoy and honor with our lives. Besides hoping to emphasize the contemporary function of black poetry, I have selected these poems according to the dictates of my heart and according to the usual criteria of excellence. May these poems challenge the daily language of our intercourse— victoriously.

In faith,
June Meyer Jordan
New York City
1969

SOULSCRIPT

TOMORROW WORDS TODAY

*

(POETRY WRITTEN BY POETS AGES 12–18)

When they write poetry, the very young brothers and sisters predict the future terms for measuring the world we must share. We can begin that next-world sharing here, as we learn the poems of ten younger Afro-American poets. Here we can examine the wonderful and early life of most-personal vocabulary: these poems.

Reflections
VANESSA HOWARD

If the world looked in a looking glass,
It'd see back hate, it'd see back war and it'd see
    back sorrow,
it'd see back fear.
If the world looked in a looking glass, it'd run
away with shame, and hide.

Monument in Black

VANESSA HOWARD

Put my black father on the penny
put his smile at me on the silver dime
put my mother on the dollar
for they've suffered for more
than three eternities of time
and all money couldn't repay

make a monument of my grandfather
let him stand in Washington
For he's suffered more than three light years
standing idle in the dark
hero of wars that weren't begun

name a holiday for my brother
on a sunny day peaceful and warm
for he's fighting for freedom
he won't be granted
all my black brothers in Vietnam
resting in unkept graves.

Foxey Lady
PHILLIP SOLOMON

Foxey lady walkin' down the street
shaking her thumbs in time with the beat,
Men's eyes poppin' out,
while little boys shout.
Hypnotizing half a street block,
half a flock of men come running,
stunning every one of them.
A path in the ground opens up
to a beautiful shell
going through the ground,
next stop "hell."

Epilogue

STEPHEN KWARTLER

bewildered souls
i've looked upon,
condemned; they lie unmoved.
        twisted,
        crumbled,
done away with,
        though never once betraying;
feeling not that i,
but that someone,
        sometime,
        crawled,
and had beaten all.

I am waiting
MICHAEL GOODE

I am waiting
    for love
I am waiting
    for happiness
I am waiting
    for a person to call my own
I am waiting, waiting
    for a fantasy
    a world of things unknown to man

Yes
I am waiting
    for things that can never be fulfilled
    never
I am waiting for a wallet as fat as the president's
Someday yes someday
    before I die.

Yes, I am poor and unworthy
    but I can dream.

April 4, 1968

MICHAEL GOODE

war war
why do god's children fight among each other
like animals
a great man once lived
a Negro man
his name was the Rev. Martin Luther King.

but do you know what happened
he was assassinated by a white man
a man of such knowledge as he
Martin Luther King
a man of such courage
to stand up and let a man hit him
without hitting back

yes
that's courage
when you fight back of course you're brave
but do you think you yourself can stand up
and let someone beat you
without batting an eyelash
that takes courage.

shot him down
that's right
one of god's children
well you can count on a long hot summer
one of our black leaders has been killed

murdered
down into the gutter.

I will long remember this dark day.

it's funny it's so you can't even
walk out in the street anymore
some maniac might shoot you
in cold blood.

what kind of a world is this?

I don't know.

death prosecuting

LINDA CURRY

death prosecuting life born
freedom slave today tomorrow
yesterday day before
O what a life i have lived

No Way Out
LINDA CURRY

the world is moving close to me
i don't know where to hide
where to run
no way out

black and white
wanting to fight
no way out

see a hole is blocked up
no way out

a world of mysteries
a world of killing
no way out

a world of unfaithful living
no way out

a world of slavery
a world of hatred and disgust

one way out
die

Hands
GLEN THOMPSON

Hands of all nations
stretching to pull one another together
pushing and lifting
the weight of hatred and greed.

Hands, hands of all colors
clasping each other in vain
trying to pull together
what's left of the world

and suddenly . . .

The hands are broken
each finger broken
by the hammer of greed and power
and of hatred and blood
and slowly the world breaks up,
pieces float to nowhere

The hands are gone
                forever

The air is dirty
GLEN THOMPSON

The air is dirty,
the streets are dirty,
the water is dirty,
half the people are dirty,
you call this living?

You see the ugly houses,
you breathe the ugly air,
you walk the ugly streets,
you hear the ugly noises,
and call it living?

You can call it living if you like,
But I don't dig it and I'm going to
split from it and I'm going to

Breathe fresh air,
walk clean streets,
meet good friends,
listen to sweet sounds,
and live, live, live

Dedication to the Final Confrontation
DJANGATOLUM (LLOYD CORBIN)

young niggers
die old
sleep nights
in days
days in
in night
sleep niggers
sleep
until
the power
of the
night
rest
get strong
niggers
get strong
eat niggers
eat
(surplus peanut butter relief etc.)
to
do
what
others might
kill
kind
man
man-kind
white
kind
of man

tripart

GAYL JONES

1.

a very friendly
prison
this is—
white kids discussing politics
and suddenly your nerves have a finished
form (half-digested rage)—
white power goes in and out of Kennedy airport
flight unknown

2.

the telephone keeps ringing
the cop keeps swinging his nightstick
and conversing with negroes
(and never knows they are blackmen)
Who is Uncle Thomas?
a nigger with pocket money.

3.

connecticut has trees
and white has two faces:
may you go to Chicago when you die.
i'll be in Harlem with Allah's
blessings
in a restaurant
dealing with humanity

Many Die Here

GAYL JONES

Many die here.
I follow the footprints of strangers
to the tombs of strangers.
I squat with cupped hands.
To the living people
my back is turned.
I look to Zen for validation
I look to the three christs:
but there are trucks in the forest
loaded down with carcasses.
there are naked children
running, dancing toward the water,
splashing being baptized by their unknown
fathers
i, who have revoked all ritual,
picking prayers from my teeth,
i see the shining lake and the
cool children:
my god is a black giant.
i slid down the rocks
with mud in my mouth,
herding the cattle and goats of others.
i met a bearded man
who said, "You are young,
but you have the spirit of the dead;
learn from me; learn from the
living people."
i answered, "You are one who

will soon have to do the dying."
(nests, hanging empty
skulls of birds
the man, in old sandals)

i laugh and laugh:

when you are old and without place or people
i will come riding my donkey along the road
to annoy you with its braying.
You, who have let my people die without a name.

Satori

GAYL JONES

disturbed by consciousness
god created creation
he traced our lives in ink
ink is made of soot and glue
and the old man sits with
an empty mind:
this is Buddhahood
this is the second christ
(Is He still alive?
Yes.
How old is He?
Eighty.
He's still a child.)

we pray over our beer
and i spring from the
Buddha's forehead,
black as jesus.

ALL ABOUT THE ALWAYS FIRST

✳

(HOMEPOETRY)

*Before anyone else, we know
the homepeople of our natural
family. Before anywhere else,
we exist inside the family
terrain, the family circumstance
of shelter. Here are Afro-American
poems of homeplace written to
the homepeople of every natural
heart: poems to the parents, the children,
the brothers and the sisters.*

———

My People
LANGSTON HUGHES

The night is beautiful,
So the faces of my people.

The stars are beautiful,
So the eyes of my people.

Beautiful, also, is the sun.
Beautiful, also, are the souls of my people.

Mother to Son

LANGSTON HUGHES

Well, son, I'll tell you:
Life for me ain't been no crystal stair.
It's had tacks in it,
And splinters,
And boards torn up,
And places with no carpet on the floor—
Bare.
But all the time
I'se been a-climbin' on,
And reachin' landin's,
And turnin' corners,
And sometimes goin' in the dark
Where there ain't been no light.
So boy, don't you turn back.
Don't you set down on the steps
'Cause you find it's kinder hard.
Don't you fall now—
For I'se still goin', honey,
I'se still climbin',
And life for me ain't been no crystal stair.

Fruit of the Flower
COUNTEE CULLEN

My father is a quiet man
With sober, steady ways
For simile, a folded fan,
His nights are like his days.

My mother's life is puritan,
No hint of cavalier,
A pool so calm you're sure it can
Have little depth to fear.

And yet my father's eyes can boast
How full his life has been;
There haunts them yet the languid ghost
Of some still sacred sin.

And though my mother chants of God,
And of the mystic river,
I've seen a bit of checkered sod
Set all her flesh aquiver.

Why should he deem it pure mischance
A son of his is fain
To do a naked tribal dance
Each time he hears the rain?

Why should she think it devil's art
That all my songs should be
Of love and lovers, broken heart,
And wild sweet agony?

Who plants a seed begets a bud,
Extract of that same root;
Why marvel at the hectic blood
That flushes this wild fruit?

Those Winter Sundays
ROBERT HAYDEN

Sundays too my father got up early
and put his clothes on in the blueblack cold,
then with cracked hands that ached
from labor in the weekday weather made
banked fires blaze. No one ever thanked him.

I'd wake and hear the cold splintering, breaking.
When the rooms were warm, he'd call,
and slowly I would rise and dress,
fearing the chronic angers of that house,

Speaking indifferently to him,
who had driven out the cold
and polished my good shoes as well.
What did I know, what did I know
of love's austere and lonely offices?

NIKKI-ROSA
NIKKI GIOVANNI

childhood remembrances are always a drag
if you're Black
you always remember things like living in Woodlawn
with no inside toilet
and if you become famous or something
they never talk about how happy you were to have your mother
all to yourself and
how good the water felt when you got your bath from one of
those big tubs that folk in chicago barbecue in
and somehow when you talk about home
it never gets across how much you
understood their feelings
as the whole family attended meetings about Hollydale
and even though you remember
your biographers never understand
your father's pain as he sells his stock
and another dream goes
and though you're poor it isn't poverty that
concerns you
and though they fought a lot
it isn't your father's drinking that makes any difference
but only that everybody is together and you
and your sister have happy birthdays and very good christmasses
and I really hope no white person ever has cause to write
about me because they never understand Black love is Black
wealth and they'll probably talk about my hard childhood
and never understand that all the while I was quite happy

The Bean Eaters
GWENDOLYN BROOKS

They eat beans mostly, this old yellow pair.
Dinner is a casual affair.
Plain chipware on a plain and creaking wood,
Tin flatware.

Two who are Mostly Good.
Two who have lived their day,
But keep on putting on their clothes
And putting things away.

And remembering . . .
Remembering, with twinklings and twinges,
As they lean over the beans in their rented back room that
    is full of beads and receipts and dolls and cloths,
    tobacco crumbs, vases and fringes.

On the Birth of My Son, Malcolm Coltrane

JULIUS LESTER

(AT THE TIME OF THE NEWARK REBELLION JULY 12, 1967)

Even as we kill,
let us
not
forget
that it is only so we may be
more human.

Let our
exaltations not be
for the blood that
flows in the gutters,
but for the
blood that
may more freely flow through our bodies.

We must
kill
in order to live,
but let us never
enjoy the
killing
more than the
new life,
the only reason for the killing.

And if we forget,
then those who come

Afterward
will have to kill us
(will have to kill us)
for the
life that we,
in our killing,
failed
to give them.

Award

RAY DUREM

A Gold Watch to the FBI Man who
has followed me for 25 Years.

Well, old spy
looks like I
led you down some pretty blind alleys,
took you on several trips to Mexico,
fishing in the high Sierras,
jazz at the Philharmonic.
You've watched me all your life,
I've clothed your wife,
put your two sons through college.
what good has it done?
the sun keeps rising every morning.
ever see me buy an Assistant President?
or close a school?
or lend money to Trujillo?
ever catch me rigging airplane prices?
I bought some after-hours whiskey in L.A.
but the Chief got his pay.
I ain't killed no Koreans
or fourteen-year-old boys in Mississippi.
neither did I bomb Guatemala,
or lend guns to shoot Algerians.
I admit I took a Negro child
to a white rest room in Texas,
but she was my daughter, only three,
who had to pee.

Five winters age
DAVID HENDERSON

Five winters age
—footfall of memory, the overriding thrust—
When boy asked mother the way of salvation before need,
the way to escape forfeit and rebalance: the short cut
to the red berries.
Ten winters march away in broken file.
The drift of their memory sways, the knob
of love warped in memory and metaphor.
Ten winters hence when the boy asked the first fastest Maiden
What, was, and, why, where?
When the boy knew and wasn't sure and the maiden recited
the verse of her life.

     on the first day an illegitimate girl
     was born to a black woman who in health stalked
     the streets cloaked in her subterranean fury of finery
     in search of love or Olympus
     Hence that woman in her windy and ceaseless flight
     from the South—her yellow skin blazing the sown
     lust of her birth. (Irish white man, Black Black woman).
     after Emancipation and Blood-soiree
     the ready room of the south ignobled a half-sister
     (not in Law but in concupiscence forward) and this
     sister in her flight carved her alabaster space from
     stone and black-blood shed in leisure.

In the worn crotch of the alabaster moment the connection
of the void that for a single purpose is multi-purposed.

Uncle Bull-boy

JUNE JORDAN

His brother   after dinner
once a year would play the piano
short and tough in white shirt
plaid suspenders   green tie and
checked trousers.
Two teeth were gold.   His eyes
were pink with alcohol.   His fingers
thumped for Auld Lang Syne.
He played St. Louis Woman
Boogie, Blues, the light
pedestrian.

          But one night   after dinner
after chitterlings and pigs' feet
after bourbon rum and rye
after turnip greens and mustard greens
and sweet potato pie
Bullboy looking everywhere
realized his brother was not there.

Who would emphasize the luxury
of ice cream by the gallon who would
repeat effusively the glamour not the gall
of five degrees outstanding on the wall?
Which head would nod and then recall
the crimes   the apples stolen from the stalls
the soft coal stolen by the pile?
Who would admire

the eighteenth pair of forty
dollar shoes?
Who could extol their mother with good
brandy as his muse?

His brother   dead from drinking
Bullboy drank to clear his thinking
saw the roach inside the riddle.
Soon the bubbles from his glass
were the only bits of charm
which overcame his folded arms.

To My Son Parker, Asleep in the Next Room
BOB KAUFMAN

On ochre walls in ice-formed caves shaggy Neanderthals
    marked their place in time.
On germinal trees in equatorial stands embryonic giants
    carved beginnings.
On Tasmanian flatlands mud-clothed first men hacked rock,
    still soft.
On Melanesian mountain peaks barked heads were reared
    in pride and beauty.
On steamy Java's cooling lava stooped humans raised
    stones to altar height.
On newborn China's plain mythless sons of Han acquired
    peaked gods with teak faces.
On holy India's sacred soil future gods carved worshipped
    reflections.
On Coptic Ethiopia's pimple rock pyramid builders tore
    volcanoes from earth.
On death-loving Egypt's godly sands living sacrifices
    carved naked power.
On Sumeria's cliffs speechless artists gouged messages
    to men yet uncreated.
On glorious Assyria's earthen dens art priests chipped
    figures of awe and hidden dimensions.
On splendored Peru's god-stained body filigreed temples
    were torn from severed hands.
On perfect Greece's bloody sites marble stirred
    under hands of men.
On degenerate Rome's trembling sod imitators sculpted lies
    into beauty.

On slave Europe's prostrate form chained souls shaped
free men.
On wild America's green torso original men painted
glacial languages.
On cold Arctica's snowy surface leathery men raised
totems in frozen air.
On this shore, you are all men, before, forever,
eternally free in all things.
On this short, we shall raise our monuments of stones,
of wood, of mud, of color, of labor, of
belief, of being, of life, of love,
of self, of man expressed in self-determined
compliance, or willful revolt,
secure in this avowed truth, that no
man is our master, nor can any ever
be, at any time in time to come.

Song of the Son

JEAN TOOMER

Pour O pour that parting soul in song,
O pour it in the sawdust glow of night,
Into the velvet pine-smoke air tonight,
And let the valley carry it along.
And let the valley carry it along.

O land and soil, red soil and sweet-gum tree,
So scant of grass, so profligate of pines,
Now just before an epoch's sun declines
Thy son, in time, I have returned to thee,
Thy son, I have, in time, returned to thee.

In time, for though the sun is setting on
A song-lit race of slaves, it has not set;
Though late, O soil, it is not too late yet
To catch thy plaintive soul, leaving, soon gone,
Leaving, to catch thy plaintive soul soon gone.

O Negro slaves, dark purple ripened plums,
Squeezed, and bursting in the pine-wood air,
Passing, before they strip the old tree bare
One plum was saved for me, one seed becomes

An everlasting song, a singing tree,
Caroling softly souls of slavery,
What they were, and what they are to me,
Caroling softly souls of slavery.

Preface to a Twenty Volume Suicide Note
LEROI JONES

Lately, I've become accustomed to the way
The ground opens up and envelops me
Each time I go out to walk the dog.
Or the broad edged silly music the wind
Makes when I run for a bus—

Things have come to that.

And now, each night I count the stars,
And each night I get the same number.
And when they will not come to be counted
I count the holes they leave.

Nobody sings anymore.

And then last night, I tiptoed up
To my daughter's room and heard her
Talking to someone, and when I opened
The door, there was no one there . . .
Only she on her knees,
Peeking into her own clasped hands.

HERO HYMNS
AND HEROINES

*

We enter a history of
victorious struggle thanks
to a deeply amazing number of
men and women whose lives
we must honor with our own.
This is the poetry of tribute—
as privilege and as powerful
obligation.

Blues Note

BOB KAUFMAN

Ray Charles is the black wind of Kilimanjaro,
Screaming up-and-down blues,
Moaning happy on all the elevators of my time.

Smiling into the camera, with an African symphony
Hidden in his throat, and (*I Got a Woman*) wails, too.

He burst from Bessie's crushed black skull
One cold night outside of Nashville, shouting,
And grows bluer from memory, glowing bluer, still.

At certain times you can see the moon
Balanced on his head.

From his mouth he hurls chunks of raw soul.
He separated the sea of polluted sounds
And led the blues into the Promised Land.

Ray Charles is a dangerous man ('way cross town),
And I love him.

(FOR RAY CHARLES'S BIRTHDAY *N.Y.C.* / *1961*)

At That Moment

RAYMOND R. PATTERSON

(For Malcolm X)

When they shot Malcolm Little down
On the stage of the Audubon Ballroom,
When his life ran out through bullet holes
(Like the people running out when the murder began)
His blood soaked the floor
One drop found a crack through the stark
Pounding thunder—slipped under the stage and began
Its journey: burrowed through concrete into the cellar,
Dropped down darkness, exploding like quicksilver
Pellets of light, panicking rats, paralyzing cockroaches—
Tunneled through rubble and wrecks of foundations,
The rocks that buttress the bowels of the city, flowed
Into pipes and powerlines, the mains and cables of the city:
A thousand fiery seeds.
At that moment,
Those who drank water where he entered . . .
Those who cooked food where he passed . . .
Those who burned light while he listened . . .
Those who were talking as he went, knew he was water
Running out of faucets, gas running out of jets, power
Running out of sockets, meaning running along taut wires—
To the hungers of their living. It is said
Whole slums of clotted Harlem plumbing groaned

And sundered free that day, and disconnected gas and light
Went on and on and on. . . .
They rushed his riddled body on a stretcher
To the hospital. But the police were too late.
It had already happened.

Runagate Runagate
ROBERT HAYDEN

1.

Runs falls rises stumbles on from darkness into darkness
and the darkness thicketed with shapes of terror
and the hunters pursuing and the hounds pursuing
and the night cold and the night long and the river
to cross and the jack-muh-lanterns beckoning beckoning
and blackness ahead and when shall I reach that somewhere
morning and keep on going and never turn back and keep on going

                Runagate
                        Runagate
                                Runagate

Many thousands rise and go
many thousands crossing over

                                        O mythic North
                                O star-shaped yonder Bible city

Some go weeping and some rejoicing
some in coffins and some in carriages
some in silks and some in shackles

                Rise and go or fare you well

No more auction block for me
no more driver's lash for me

If you see my Pompey, 30 yrs of age,
new breeches, plain stockings, negro shoes;
if you see my Anna, likely young mulatto
branded E on the right cheek, R on the left,
catch them if you can and notify subscriber.
Catch them if you can, but it won't be easy.
They'll dart underground when you try to catch them,
plunge into quicksand, whirlpools, mazes,
turn into scorpions when you try to catch them.

And before I'll be a slave
I'll be buried in my grave

North star and bonanza gold
I'm bound for the freedom, freedom-bound
and oh Susyanna don't you cry for me

Runagate

Runagate

II.
Rises from their anguish and their power,
Harriet Tubman,

woman of earth, whipscarred,
a summoning, a shining

Mean to be free

And this was the way of it, brethren brethren,
way we journeyed from Can't to Can.
Moon so bright and no place to hide,
the cry up and the patterollers riding,
hound dogs belling in bladed air.
And fear starts a-murbling, Never make it,
we'll never make it. *Hush that now,*
and she's turned upon us, levelled pistol
glinting in the moonlight:
Dead folks can't jaybird-talk, she says;
you keep on going now or die, she says.

Wanted   Harriet Tubman   alias The General
alias Moses   Stealer of Slaves

In league with Garrison   Alcott   Emerson
Garrett   Douglass   Thoreau   John Brown
Armed and known to be Dangerous

Wanted   Reward   Dead or Alive

Tell me, Ezekiel, oh tell me do you see
mailed Jehovah coming to deliver me?

Hoot-owl calling in the ghosted air,
five times calling to the hants in the air.
Shadow of a face in the scary leaves,
shadow of a voice in the talking leaves:

Come ride-a my train

Oh that train, ghost-story train
through swamp and savanna movering movering,
over trestles of dew, through caves of the wish,
Midnight Special on a sabre track movering movering,
first stop Mercy and the last Hallelujah.

Come ride-a my train

Mean mean mean to be free.

Frederick Douglass
ROBERT HAYDEN

When it is finally ours, this freedom, this liberty, this beautiful
and terrible thing, needful to man as air,
usable as earth; when it belongs at last to all,
when it is truly instinct, brain matter, diastole, systole,
reflex action; when it is finally won; when it is more
than the gaudy mumbo jumbo of politicians:
this man, this Douglass, this former slave, this Negro
beaten to his knees, exiled, visioning a world
where none is lonely, none hunted, alien,
this man, superb in love and logic, this man
shall be remembered. Oh, not with statues' rhetoric,
not with legends and poems and wreaths of bronze alone,
but with the lives grown out of his life, the lives
fleshing his dream of the beautiful, needful thing.

Malcolm X—an Autobiography

LARRY NEAL

I am the Seventh Son of the Son
who was also the Seventh.
I have drunk deep of the waters of my ancestors
have traveled the soul's journey towards cosmic harmony
the Seventh Son.
Have walked slick avenues
and seen grown men, fall, to die in a blue doom
of death and ancestral agony,
have seen old men glide, shadowless, feet barely
touching the pavements.

I sprung out of the Midwestern plains
the bleak Michigan landscape wearing the slave name—
　　Malcolm Little.
Saw a brief vision in Lansing, when I was seven, and in
my mother's womb heard the beast cry of death,
a landscape on which white robed figures ride, and my
Garvey father silhouetted against the night-fire, gun in hand
form outlined against a panorama of violence.

Out of the midwestern bleakness, I sprang, pushed eastward,
past shack on country nigger shack, across the wilderness
of North America.
I hustler. I pimp. I unfulfilled black man
bursting with destiny.
New York city Slim called me Big Red,
and there was no escape, close nights of the smell of death.
Pimp. Hustler. The day fills these rooms.

I am talking about New York. Harlem.
talking about the neon madness.
talking about ghetto eyes and nights
about death oozing across the room. Small's paradise.
talking about cigarette butts, and rooms smelly with white
sex flesh, and dank sheets, and being on the run.
talking about cocaine illusions, about stealing and selling.
talking about these New York cops who smell of blood and money.
I am Big Red, tiger vicious, Big Red, bad nigger, will kill.

But there is rhythm here. Its own special substance:
I hear Billie sing, no good man, and dig Prez, wearing the Zoot
suit of life, the pork-pie hat tilted at the correct angle.
through the Harlem smoke of beer and whiskey, I understand the
mystery of the signifying monkey,
in a blue haze of inspiration, I reach for the totality of Being.
I am at the center of a swirl of events. War and death.
rhythm. hot women. I think life a commodity bargained for
across the bar in Small's.
I perceive the echoes of Bird and there is gnawing in the maw
of my emotions.

and then there is jail. America is the world's greatest jailer,
and we all in jails. Black spirits contained like magnificent
birds of wonder. I now understand my father urged on by the
ghost of Garvey,
and see a small black man standing in a corner. The cell, cold.
dank. The light around him vibrates. Am I crazy? But to under-
stand is to submit to a more perfect will, a more perfect order,
to understand is to surrender the imperfect self,
for a more perfect self.

Allah formed man, I follow
and shake within the very depth of my most imperfect being,
and I bear witness to the Message of Allah
and I bear witness—all praise is due Allah!

In Time of Crisis

RAYMOND R. PATTERSON

You are the brave who do not break
In the grip of the mob when the blow comes straight
To the shattered bone; when the sockets shriek;
When your arms lie twisted under your back.

Good men holding their courage slack
In their frightened pockets see how weak
The work that is done—and feel the weight
Of your blood on the ground for their spirits' sake;

And build their anger, stone on stone—
Each silently, but not alone.

The Ballad of Rudolph Reed
GWENDOLYN BROOKS

Rudolph Reed was oaken.
His wife was oaken too.
And his two good girls and his good little man
Oakened as they grew.

"I am not hungry for berries.
I am not hungry for bread.
But hungry hungry for a house
Where at night a man in bed

"May never hear the plaster
Stir as if in pain.
May never hear the roaches
Falling like fat rain.

"Where never wife and children need
Go blinking through the gloom.
Where every room of many rooms
Will be full of room.

"Oh my home may have its east or west
Or north or south behind it.
All I know is I shall know it,
And fight for it when I find it."

It was in a street of bitter white
That he made his application.
For Rudolph Reed was oakener
Than others in the nation.

The agent's steep and steady stare
Corroded to a grin.
Why, you black old, tough old hell of a man,
Move your family in!

Nary a grin grinned Rudolph Reed,
Nary a curse cursed he,
But moved in his House. With his dark little wife,
And his dark little children three.

A neighbor would *look*, with a yawning eye
That squeezed into a slit.
But the Rudolph Reeds and the children three
Were too joyous to notice it.

For were they not firm in a home of their own
With windows everywhere
And a beautiful banistered stair
And a front yard for flowers and a back yard for grass?

The first night, a rock, big as two fists.
The second, a rock big as three.
But nary a curse cursed Rudolph Reed.
(Though oaken as man could be.)

The third night, a silvery ring of glass.
Patience ached to endure.
But he looked, and lo! small Mabel's blood
Was staining her gaze so pure.

Then up did rise our Rudolph Reed
and pressed the hand of his wife,

And went to the door with a thirty-four
And a beastly butcher knife.

He ran like a mad thing to the night.
And the words in his mouth were stinking.
By the time he had hurt his first white man
He was no longer thinking.

By the time he had hurt his fourth white man
Rudolph Reed was dead.
His neighbors gathered and kicked his corpse.
"Nigger—" his neighbors said.

Small Mabel whimpered all night long,
For calling herself the cause.
Her oak-eyed mother did no thing
But change the bloody gauze.

Blind and Deaf Old Woman
CLARENCE MAJOR

spots on black skin
.   She is dry.   This steel dust
how time, how she waits here
dingywool shabby, the fingers on the cup her
frail
                woven face, oval black
empty charity
.   She remains quiet, please.   The cup
shape)
(
        shakes. It is not straight, no-
thing is.
        She does not sell
candy &
rubber bands like the.
                        Silence, the sounds
    .Of grotesque pennies
into O. /bent
    .Up her canvas stool, she
returns thru
                    these Indiana 1960 streets.
    Folds up her silence,
shuffles   into street sounds.

After Winter
STERLING A. BROWN

He snuggles his fingers
In the blacker loam
The lean months are done with,
The fat to come.

His eyes are set
On a brushwood-fire
But his heart is soaring
Higher and higher.

Though he stands ragged
An old scarecrow,
This is the way
His swift thoughts go,

"Butter beans fo' Clara
Sugar corn fo' Grace
An' fo' de little feller
Runnin' space.

"Radishes and lettuce
Eggplants and beets
Turnips fo' de winter
An' candied sweets.

"Homespun tobacco
Apples in de bin
Fo' smokin' an' fo' cider
When de folks draps in."

He thinks with the winter
His troubles are gone;
Ten acres unplanted
To raise dreams on.

The lean months are done with,
The fat to come.
His hopes, winter wanderers,
Hasten home.

"Butterbeans fo' Clara
Sugar corn fo' Grace
An' fo' de little feller
Runnin' space. . . ."

Holyghost Woman: An Ole Nomad Moving Thru the South

CLARENCE MAJOR

pre-
tending not to BE
not even flesh wind talked in her way of
looking transient: DECEPTION spoke out of
stride, the petty quiver   HIGHER!!!   : cause
coming on a flat devotion to a
disrespectful glory, she was glory
—as god's agent, not even herself knowing
whether/or NOT "it
(is

but commercial, material: her soft flirting
with the instability of all these
      DEVOUTLY RE: RE-
ligious "souls" taste cajolery itself in
       (((SOOOOOO MUCH RARE HUGE
       MYSTERY TABOO)))
that off this Georgia highway she catches the sun
just right, near a shack meet voices black
so BLACK & SOFT gentle honeysweet trusting these
humble people I know so
well & ready to give to her, a woman called Sister
Patty Johnson (ex-slave to nothing but MOTION:)
      EVERYTHING: in the midday of silver leaves
from the moment of the front porch, EVERY-
THING they had to give she ATE, hard.

Second Avenue Encounter
RAYMOND R. PATTERSON

The old guy cursed me for the coin I held—
Etched with his lone, shark's tooth a yellow poem,
Catching my startled soul on the thorn of his tongue.

Blocking my path, that reeking jaw of pain
Cursed me and mocked me; my necktie-knotted throat,
My thoughtless mornings slipping into suits,
My sliding into shoes that always fit—
Hoisting his leg and wagging the wretched stump
As how he grubs toward death up to his groin;

Cursed my disease. So brought to my knees I cried,
"May God forgive me! I am betrayed like you!"
And kissed him where his cheek was wet with dew,
And dropped my coin into his wounded side.

If you saw a Negro lady

JUNE JORDAN

If you saw a Negro lady
sitting on a Tuesday
near the whirl-sludge doors of
Horn & Hardart on the main drag
of downtown Brooklyn

solitary and conspicuous as plain
and neat as walls impossible to
fresco and you watched her self-
conscious features shape about
a Horn & Hardart teaspoon
with a pucker from a cartoon

she would not understand
with spine as straight and solid
as her years of bending over floors
allowed

skin cleared of interest by a ruthless
soap   nails square and yellowclean
from metal files

sitting in a forty-year-old flush
of solitude and prickling
from the new white cotton blouse
concealing nothing she had ever noticed
even when she bathed and never
hummed a bathtub tune nor knew one

If you saw her square
above the dirty
mopped-on antiseptic floors
before the rag-wiped table tops

little finger   broad and stiff
in heavy emulation of a cockney

mannerism

would you turn her treat
into surprise observing
happy birthday

CORNERS ON THE CURVING SKY

✳

*Our earth is round and, among
other things, that means that
you and I can hold completely
different points of view and
both be right. The difference
of our positions will show stars
in your window I cannot even
imagine. Your sky may burn with
light, while mine, at the same
moment, spreads beautiful to
darkness. Still, we must choose
how we separately corner the
circling universe of our experience.
Once chosen, our concerning will
determine the message of any star
and darkness we encounter.
These poems speak to philosophy;
they reveal the corners where we
organize what we know.*

American Gothic

PAUL VESEY

To Satch

(The legendary Satchel Paige, one of the star pitchers in Negro baseball)

Sometimes I feel like I will *never* stop
Just go on forever
Til one fine mornin'

I'm gonna reach up and grab me a handfulla stars
Swing out my long lean leg
And whip three hot strikes burnin' down the heavens
And look over at God and say
How about that!

Counterpoint

OWEN DODSON

Terror does not belong to open day

Picnics on the beach, all along
The unmined water children play,
A merry-go-round begins a jingle song,
Horses churn up and down the peppermint poles,
Children reach for the brassy ring,
Children laugh while the platform rolls
Faster and faster while the horses sing:

merry-ro, merry-o,
this is the way your lives should go:
up and down and all around
listening to this merry sound.

Terror does not belong to open day

merry-ro, merry-ha,
snatch this ring and plant a star;
grow a field of magic light,
reap it on a winter night.

Terror does not belong to open day

The Creation

JAMES WELDON JOHNSON

And God stepped out on space,
And he looked around and said:
I'm lonely—
I'll make me a world.

And far as the eye of God could see
Darkness covered everything,
Blacker than a hundred midnights
Down in a cypress swamp.

Then God smiled,
And the light broke,
And the darkness rolled up on one side,
And the light stood shining on the other,
And God said: That's good!

Then God reached out and took the light in his hands,
And God rolled the light around in his hands
Until he made the sun;
And he set that sun a-blazing in the heavens.
And the light that was left from making the sun
God gathered it up in a shining ball
And flung it against the darkness,
Spangling the night with the moon and stars.
Then down between
The darkness and the light
He hurled the world;
And God said: That's good!

Then God himself stepped down—
And the sun was on his right hand,
And the moon was on his left;
The stars were clustered about his head,
And the earth was under his feet.
And God walked, and where he trod
His footsteps hollowed the valleys out
And bulged the mountains up.

Then he stopped and looked and saw
That the earth was hot and barren.
So God stepped over to the edge of the world
And he spat out the seven seas—
He batted his eyes, and the lightnings flashed—
He clapped his hands, and the thunders rolled—
And the waters above the earth came down,
The cooling waters came down.

Then the green grass sprouted,
And the little red flowers blossomed,
The pine tree pointed his finger to the sky,
And the oak spread out his arms,
The lakes cuddled down in the hollows of the ground,
And the rivers ran down to the sea;
And God smiled again,
And the rainbow appeared,
And curled itself around his shoulder.

Then God raised his arm and he waved his hand
Over the sea and over the land,
And he said: Bring forth! Bring forth!

And quicker than God could drop his hand,
Fishes and fowls
And beasts and birds
Swam the rivers and the seas,
Roamed the forests and the woods,
And split the air with their wings.
And God said: That's good!

Then God walked around,
And God looked around
On all that he had made.
He looked at his sun,
And he looked at his moon,
And he looked at his little stars;
He looked on his world
With all its living things,
And God said: I'm lonely still.

Then God sat down—
On the side of a hill where he could think;
By a deep, wide river he sat down;
With his head in his hands,
God thought and thought,
Till he thought: I'll make me a man!

Up from the bed of the river
God scooped the clay;
And by the bank of the river
He kneeled him down;
And there the Great God Almighty
Who lit the sun and fixed it in the sky,
Who flung the stars to the most far corner of the night,

Who rounded the earth in the middle of his hand;
This Great God,
Like a mammy bending over her baby,
Kneeled down in the dust
Toiling over a lump of clay
Till he shaped it in his own image;

Then into it he blew the breath of life,
And man became a living soul.
Amen   Amen.

Reapers

JEAN TOOMER

Black reapers with the sound of steel on stones
Are sharpening scythes. I seem them place the hones
In their hip-pockets as a thing that's done,
And start their silent swinging, one by one.
Black horses drive a mower through the weeds,
And there, a field rat, startled, squealing bleeds,
His belly close to ground. I see the blade,
Blood-stained, continue cutting weeds and shade.

beware: do not read this poem

ISHMAEL REED

tonite , thriller was
abt an ol woman , so vain she
surrounded herself w/
    many mirrors

it got so bad that finally she
locked herself indoors & her
whole life became the
    mirrors

one day the villagers broke
into her house , but she was too
swift for them . she disappeared
    into a mirror
each tenant who bought the house
after that , lost a loved one to
    the ol woman in the mirror :
    first a little girl
    then a young woman
    then the young woman/s husband

the hunger of this poem is legendary
it has taken in many victims
back off from this poem
it has drawn in yr feet
back off from this poem
it has drawn in yr legs

back off from this poem
it is a greedy mirror
you are into his poem . from
    the waist down
nobody can hear you can they ?
this poem has had you up to here
    belch
this poem aint got no manners
you cant call out frm this poem
relax now & go w/ this poem
move & roll on to this poem
do not resist this poem
this poem has yr eyes
this poem has his head
this poem has his arms
this poem has his fingers
this poem has his fingertips

this poem is the reader & the
reader this poem

statistic : the us bureau of missing persons reports
            that in 1968 over 100,000 people disappeared
            leaving no solid clues
                    nor trace   only
a space   in the lives of their friends

Mud in Vietnam
JULIUS LESTER

Vietnam is
muddy
backroads
through hamlets that
had
no roads
(not even for ox-cart)
in the time of the French,
when thatched huts were
scattered through
fields
that were deserts in dry season,
lakes where no fish swam in rainy season.
Vietnam is
muddy
backroads
between the
canals
and
the
rice-fields
that are
green
green
green
a
gentle
undulating
green

(where there are no 15 foot deep bomb craters)
that will
grow into a
playful
yellow
at harvest time.

Vietnam is
muddy
backroads
that
splatter the clothes
as
Army trucks
hurry beneath the
ever-threatening sky
where a distant cloud may be F 105's
("We have done nothing to the Americans")
and
a life is
no more
than that of a
rice kernel
falling from a peasant's basket into
the mud
and
being stepped on.

The
mud
of
Vietnam

is
woman-thigh
deep
with backs bent,
for muddiness is next to Godliness,
woman-thigh deep
in the fields of
Hung Yen Province
carving slabs of
mud that will
be cut to
brick-size and
baked in kilns—
woman-thigh high
in water,
feet
deep
in
the
mud,
planting rice—
(with a quick
turn of the wrist
green stalks
are thrust into the mud);
woman-thigh high
midst the delicate rice
hair (tied loosely
at the back of the head)
falling below the
hips
and

brushing the tops
of the
green
rice stalks.

Their
woman-ness
seems to grow from
the
mud
of
Vietnam
where they stand,
woman-thigh high
woman-thigh deep.

I would like
to make love

woman-thigh high
woman-thigh deep
in
the
mud
of
Vietnam.

The girls, *quan dai den* rolled
Above their knees, left the fields,
Their wet legs glistened like the
Barrels of the rifles on their backs.

lxvii

JULIUS LESTER

If there were not a war,
I would smile at the acne-blemished
Kids with rifles on their backs.
        (March 24, 1967)

of faith: confessional
JUNE JORDAN

silence polishing the streets to rain
who walk the waters
side by side

or used to dance apart
a squaretoe solo stunt
apart
ran stubbornly to pantomime
a corpse

show shadows of the deafman
yesterday the breathing broke
to blow some light against the walls

tomorrow drums the body into birth
a symbol of the sun
entirely alive

a birth to darkness

furnace rioting inside the fruit-rim ribs
dogeaten at the garden gate
but better than the other
early bones

that made the dog eat dog
that made the man smash man

catastrophe

far better
better bones

establishing

a second starting
history

a happiness

Brown River, Smile

JEAN TOOMER

It is a new America,
To be spiritualized by each new American.

Lift, lift, thou waking forces!
Let us feel the energy of animals,
The energy of rumps and bull-bent heads
Crashing the barrier to man.
It must spiral on!
A million million men, or twelve men,
Must crash the barrier to the next higher form.

    Beyond plants are animals,
    Beyond animals is man,
    Beyond man is the universe.

    The Big Light,
    Let the Big Light in!

O thou, Radiant Incorporeal,
The I of earth and of mankind, hurl
Down these seaboards, across this continent,
The thousand-rayed discus of thy mind,
And above our walking limbs unfurl
Spirit-torsos of exquisite strength!

The Mississippi, sister of the Ganges,
Main artery of earth in the western world,
Is waiting to become
In the spirit of America, a sacred river.

Whoever lifts the Mississippi
Lifts himself and all America;
Whoever lifts himself
Makes that great brown river smile.
The blood of earth and the blood of man
Course swifter and rejoice when we spiritualize.

The old gods, led by an inverted Christ,
A shaved Moses, a blanched Lemur,
And a moulting thunderbird,
Withdrew into the distance and soon died,
Their dust and seed falling down
To fertilize the five regions of America.

We are waiting for a new God.

The old peoples—
The great European races sent wave after wave
That washed the forests, the earth's rich loam,
Grew towns with the seeds of giant cities,
Made roads, laid golden rails,
Sang once of its swift achievement,
And died congested in machinery.
They say that near the end
It was a world of crying men and hard women,
A city of goddam and Jehovah
Baptized in industry
Without benefit of saints,
Of dear defectives
Winnowing their likenesses from weathered rock
Sold by national organizations of undertakers.

Someone said:
    Suffering is impossible
    On cement sidewalks, in skyscrapers,
    In motorcars;
    Steel cannot suffer—
    We die unconsciously
    Because possessed by a nonhuman symbol.

Another cried:
    It is because of thee, O Life,
    That the first prayer ends in the last curse.

Another sang:
    Late minstrels of the restless earth,
    No muteness can be granted thee,
    Lift thy laughing energies
    To that white point which is a star.

The great African races sent a single wave
And singing ripplets to sorrow in red fields,
Sing a swan song, to break rocks
And immortalize a hiding water boy.

    I'm leaving the shining ground, brothers,
    I sing because I ache,
    I go because I must,
    Brothers, I am leaving the shining ground;
    Don't ask me where,
    I'll meet you there,
    I'm leaving the shining ground.

The great red race was here.
In a land of flaming earth and torrent-rains,
Of red sea-plains and majestic mesas,
At sunset from a purple hill
The Gods came down;
They serpentined into pueblo,
And a white-robed priest
Danced with them five days and nights;
But pueblo, priest, and Shalicos
Sank into the sacred earth
To fertilize the five regions of America.

    Hi-ye, hi-yo, hi-yo
    Hi-ye, hi-yo, hi-yo,
    A lone eagle feather,
    An untamed Navaho,
    The ghosts of buffaloes,
    Hi-ye, hi-yo, hi-yo,
    Hi-ye, hi-yo, hi-yo.

We are waiting for a new people.

O thou, Radiant Incorporeal,
The I of earth and of mankind, hurl
Down these seaboards, across this continent,
The thousand-rayed discus of thy mind,
And above our walking limbs unfurl
Spirit-torsos of exquisite strength!
The east coast is masculine,
The west coast is feminine,
The middle region is the child—
Forces of reconciling

And generator of symbols.
Thou, great fields, waving thy growths across the world,
Couldest thou find the seed which started thee?
Can you remember the first great hand to sow?
Have you memory of His intention?
  Great plains, and thou, mountains,
  And thou, stately trees, and thou,
  America, sleeping and producing with the seasons,
  No clever dealer can divide,
  No machine can undermine thee.

The prairie's sweep is flat infinity,
The city's rise is perpendicular to farthest star,
I stand where the two directions intersect,
At Michigan Avenue and Walton Place,
Parallel to my countrymen,
Right-angled to the universe.

It is a new America,
To be spiritualized by each new American.

The end of man is his beauty
LEROI JONES

And silence
which proves/but
a referent
to my disorder.
              Your world shakes

cities die
beneath your shape.

   The single shadow

at noon
like a live tree
whose leaves
are like clouds

Weightless soul
at whose love faith moves
as a dark and
withered day.

They speak of singing who
have never heard song; of living
whose deaths are legends
for their kind.

        A scream
gathered in wet fingers,
at the top of its stalk.

—They have passed
and gone
whom you thot your lovers

In this perfect quiet, my friend,
their shapes
are not unlike
night's

As a possible lover

LEROI JONES

Practices
silence, the way of wind
bursting
its early lull. Cold morning
to night, we go so
slowly, without
thought
to ourselves. (Enough
to have thought
tonight, nothing
finishes it. What
you are, will have
no certainty, or
end. That you will
stay, where you are,
a human gentle wisp
of life. Ah . . .)
                    practices
loneliness,
as a virtue. A single
specious need
to keep
what you have
never really
had.

This Age

RAYMOND R. PATTERSON

What year is this? Who can truthfully say?
Have we reached the middle or the end
Of the Twentieth Century?
Choose a date. But let's not pretend.
No more lying almanacs, please; no more
Bogus calendars or phony electronic clocks!
The universe is shot full of holes!
Has sprung its locks! Are we on a subway
Or a seesaw? Whose face haunts the sky?
Is it too late to die?

O the earth grinds! Time winds and unwinds
Against the living grain. What is that muffled thump, like something
    falling
Again and again? Why are we here? A different
Place? A different age? These broken instruments
Again?

All night we lie on the floor
Aware, yet cold in our catastrophe of stars.
The tired droop of your furious head
Echoing my rage. Are we already dead?
Would you believe the years? Should we debate again?
We are missing! Those constellations are our fallen tears.
Why were they shed? And who can put them back and strum the
    spheres
That we may turn to singing and to bed?

Sonnet

ALFRED A. DUCKETT

Where are we to go when this is done?
Will we slip into old, accustomed ways,
finding remembered notches, one by one?
Thrashing a hapless way through quickening haze?

Who is to know us when the end has come?
Old friends and families, but could we be
strange to the sight and stricken dumb
at visions of some pulsing memory?

Who will love us for what we used to be
who now are what we are, bitter or cold?
Who is to nurse us with swift subtlety
back to the warm and feeling human fold?

Where are we to go when this is through?
We are the war-born. What are we to do?

Madhouse

CALVIN C. HERNTON

Here is a place that is no place
And here is no place that is a place
A place somewhere beyond the reaches of time
And beyond the reaches of those who in time
Bring flowers and fruit to this place,
Yet here is a definite place
And a definite time, fixed
In a timelessness of precise vantage
From which to view flowers and view fruit
And those who come bearing them.

Those who come by Sunday's habit are weary
And kiss us half-foreign but sympathetic,
Spread and eat noisily to crack the unbearable
Silence of this place:
They do not know that something must always come
From something and that nothing must come always
From nothing, and that nothing is always a thing

To drive us mad.

SAYING THE PERSON

*

If I write a poem
organizing what I know
so that my individuality,
my special I-Am, has been
spoken as exactly as I can
speak, then that poem
is saying the person.

Number 5—December

DAVID HENDERSON

Nobody knows me
when I go round
late at night
scratching on windows
& whispering in hallways
looking for someone
who loves me in the daytime
to take me in
at night

Poem

KATHERINE L. CUESTAS

One day, a long time ago,
I planted my soul
and found that the soil changed very often.
Once it was love (that proved to be harmful)
once it was nature (that proved to be excellent, but not
steady enough for so important a task)
once it was myself (that proved to be the rockiest and
driest soil; I don't know myself well enough)
one content time it was God (it was really him all along,
but I knew it not).

One time a strong wind or something knocked my pot
and all my soil over
with my soul still in it.
I was spread over a vast area and I was griefstricken.
Some kind being (probably God again) came and
replanted my soul for me;
now I am growing, because as He replanted me,
with every pat of the soil and every drop of water
He uttered the words:

STAY ALIVE

and I did.

Song

M. CARL HOLMAN

Dressed up in my melancholy
With no place to go,
Sick as sin of inwardness
And sick of being so

I walked out on the avenue,
Eager to give my hand
To any with the health to heal
Or heart to understand.

I had not walked a city block
And met with more than ten
Before I read the testament
Stark behind each grin:

Beneath the hatbrims haunting me,
More faithful than a mirror,
The figuration of my grief,
The image of my error.

Naturally

AUDRE LORDE

Since Naturally Black is Naturally Beautiful
I must be proud
And, naturally,
Black and
Beautiful
Who always was a trifle
Yellow
And plain though proud
Before.

I've given up pomades
Having spent the summer sunning
And feeling naturally free
     (if I die of skin cancer
     oh well—one less
     black and beautiful me)
Yet no Agency spends millions
To prevent my summer tanning
And who trembles nightly
With the fear of their lily cities being swallowed
By a summer ocean of naturally woolly hair?

But I've bought my can of
Natural Hair Spray
Made and marketed in Watts
Still thinking more
Proud beautiful black women
Could better make and use
Black bread.

Summer Oracle

AUDRE LORDE

Without expectation
There is no end
To the shocks of morning
Or even a small summer.

Now the image is fire
Blackening the vague lines
Into defiance across the city.
The image is fire
Sun warming us in a cold country
Barren of symbols for love.

Now I have forsaken order
And imagine you into fire
Untouchable in a magician's coat
Covered with signs of destruction and birth
Sewn with griffins and arrows and hammers
And gold sixes stitched into your hem
Your fingers draw fire
But still the old warlocks shun you
For no gourds ring in your sack
No spells bring forth peace
And I am still hungry and fruitless
This summer
The peaches are flinty and juiceless
And cry sour worms.

The image is fire
Flaming over you burning off excess

Like the blaze planters start
To burn off bagasse from the canefields
After a harvest.

The image is fire
The high sign that rules our summer.
I smell it in the charred breeze blowing over

Your body
Close
Hard
Essential
Under its cloak of lies.

IRON YEARS: *for money*

CLARENCE MAJOR

this part of the rail
,me
in these bleak hours/punching
a clock, check
the drab place, welding metal
:driving
perhaps this crane along my
line, the controls. Square
window, down on the
possibility of killing those
narrow figures
down there, ends in themselves.
Time card, out of
the overtime of this darkness
these hours, this part

off d þ*ig*
ISHMAEL REED

for f duvalier who maintained d trust

background:
    a reckoning has left
some minds hard hit   . they blow,
crying for help   , out to sea like
dead trees & receding housetops   . i
can sympathize   . i mean   , all of us
have had our dreams broken over some
body's head   . those scratched phono
graph records of d soul   .
we
            all have been zombed along
d way of a thousand eyes glowing at midnite   .
            our pupils have been vacant
            our hands have been icey &
            we have walked with a d tell tale
            lurch
all of us have had this crisis of consciousness
which didnt do nobody no good
or a search for identity
which didnt make no never mind neither

at those times we got down on our knees & call
ed up the last resort   . seldom do we bother him
for he is doing heavy duty for d universe   . only
once has he been disturbed & this was to
            put some color into a woman's blues

he came like a black fire engine spun & sped
by khepera
he is very pressed for time &
do nots play

he apologises for being late
he rolls up his sleeves & rests his bird
he starts to say a few words to d crowd   .
he sees d priests are out to lunch so he
just goes on head with what he got to do

out of d night blazing from ceciltaylor pianos
        Thoth sets down his fine black self
d first blak scribe
d one who fixes up their art
d one who draws d circle with his pen
d man who beats around d bush
d smeller outer of d fiend
                        jehovah-apep jumpo up bad on
                        d set
                        but squeals as spears bring him
                        down
a curfew is lifted on soul
friendly crowds greet one another in d streets
Osiris struts his stuff & dos d thang to words
        hidden beneath d desert
chorus—just like a legendary train that
        one has heard of but never seen
        broke all records in its prime
        takes you to where you want to go right fast

i hears you woo woo o neo american hoo doo
   church
i hears you woo woo o neo american hoo doo church
i hears you woo woo o neo american hoo doo
   church
i hears you woo woo o neo american hoo doo
   church
amen-ra   a-men ra   a-man ra

A Poem Looking for a Reader

DON L. LEE

(to be read with a love consciousness)

black is not
all inclusive,
there are other colors,
color her warm and womanly,
color her feeling and life,
color her a gibran poem and 4
    women of simone.
children will give her color
paint her the color of her
man.

most of all color her
love
a remembrance of life
a true reflection
that we
will
move u will move with

I want
u
a fifty minute call to
    blackwomanworld:
        hi baby,
            how u doin?
need u.

listening to
young-holt's, *please sunrise, please.*

to give i'll give
most personal.
what about the other
scenes: children playing in vacant lots,
     or like the first time u knowingly
          kissed a girl,
       was it joy or just beautifully beautiful.
i
remember at 13
reading chester himes'
cast the first stone and
the eyes of momma when she caught me: read on,
son.

how will u come:
     like a soulful strut in a two-piece beige o-rig'i-nal,
     or afro-down with a beat in yr/walk?
how will love come:
     painless and deep like a razor cut
     or like some cheap 75¢ movie;
     i think not.

will she be the woman
other men will want
or
will her beauty be
accented with my name on it?

she will come as she would

want her man to come.
she'll come,
she'll come.
i
never wrote a love letter
but
that doesn't mean
i
don't love.

moonlight moonlight

CLARENCE MAJOR

moonlight moonlight
in Valdosta Georgia on Moody Air Force Base. It

got: "a moon tan

from white eyes 93 inches up, on
a 45 degree angle. There was

no natural responsibility to any-
body. The night was wet, huge thick damp.

Coal

AUDRE LORDE

I
Is the total black, being spoken
From the earth's inside.
There are many kinds of open.
How a diamond comes into a knot of flame
How sound comes into a word, colored
By who pays what for speaking.

Some words are open
Like a diamond on glass windows
singing out within the crash the sun makes passing through.
There are words like stapled chances
In a perforated book—buy and sign and tear apart—
And come what wills all chances
The stub remains
An ill-pulled tooth with a ragged edge.
Some words live in my throat
Breeding like adders. Others
Know sun, seeking like gypsies over my tongue
To explode through my lips
Like young sparrows bursting from shell
Some words
Bedevil me.

Love is a word another kind of open
As a diamond comes into a know of flame
I am black because I come from the earth's inside
Take my word for jewel in your open light.

Air

CLARENCE MAJOR

breathing   the breath.   clearance   . the air
the air, the breathing air.   The math of the
    air the figures of breathing the mind
        the science of things, the
men, the life, ring repeat in/out breathing life
men give to air, the breath   . Clearance, a
clear
convincing math of things. OUT IN THE
    COUNTRY.
Trees, some irregular plants. Not here, now:
THIS CITY. of destruction to breathing, to hands
even, eyelids that cover the sounds, to lips that
pave the pavement of flesh to the air, to the
way we walk, OUT IN THE COUNTRY to get
    air. The
kind of hands that touch, break sink into soft
mud, out
there

under eyelids.

The Distant Drum
CALVIN C. HERNTON

I am not a metaphor or symbol.
This you hear is not the wind in the trees,
Nor a cat being maimed in the street.
I am being maimed in the street.
It is I who weep, laugh, feel pain or joy,
Speak this because I exist.
This is my voice.
These words are my words,
My mouth speaks them,
My hand writes—
I am a poet.
It is my fist you hear
Beating against your ear.

It's Here In The
RUSSELL ATKINS

Here in the newspaper—the wreck of the East Bound.
A photograph bound to bring on cardiac asthenia.
There is a blur that mists the page!
On one side is a gloom of dreadful harsh.
Then breaks flash lights up sheer.
There is much huge about. I suppose then
     those no's are people
   between that suffering of—
   (what more have we? for Christ's sake, no!)
Something of a full stop of it
crash of blood and the still shock
   of stark sticks and an immense swift gloss,
And two dead no's lie aghast still.
One casts a crazed eye and the other's
Closed dull.
    the heap up twists
      such
as to harden the unhard and unhard
the hardened.

This Morning
JAY WRIGHT

This morning I threw the windows
of my room open, the light burst
in like crystal gauze and I hung
it on my wall to frame.
And here I am watching it take possession
of my room, watching the obscure love
match of light and shadow—of cold and warmth.
It is a matter of acceptance, I guess.
It is a matter of finding some room
with shadows to embrace, open. Now
the light has settled in, I don't think
I shall ever close my windows again.

BLACK EYES ON
A FALLOWLAND

✳

From the time, the crimes
of slavery, America
has sacrificed the radiance
of democracy. Afro-Americans
confront the fallowland
with darkest clarity:
the clarity of their surviving,
nevertheless.
In these poems, true black eyes
look back at a land endangering
too many promises of the spirit.

———

Georgia Dusk
JEAN TOOMER

The sky, lazily disdaining to pursue
    The setting sun, too indolent to hold
    A lengthened tournament for flashing gold,
Passively darkens for night's barbecue,

A feast of moon and men and barking hounds,
    An orgy for some genius of the South
    With blood-hot eyes and cane-lipped scented mouth,
Surprised in making folk songs from soul-sounds.

The sawmill blows its whistle, buzz saws stop,
    And silence breaks the bud of knoll and hill,
    Soft settling pollen where plowed lands fulfill
Their early promise of a bumper crop.

Smoke from the pyramidal sawdust pile
    Curls up, blue ghosts of trees, tarrying low
    Where only chips and stumps are left to show
The solid proof of former domicile.

Meanwhile, the men, with vestiges of pomp,
    Race memories of king and caravan,
    High priests, an ostrich, and a juju-man,
Go singing through the footpaths of the swamp.

Their voices rise . . . the pine trees are guitars,
    Strumming, pine needles fall like sheets of rain . . .
    Their voices rise . . . the chorus of the cane
Is caroling a vesper to the stars . . .

O singers, resinous and soft your songs
    Above the sacred whisper of the pines,
    Give virgin lips to cornfield concubines,
Bring dreams of Christ to dusky cane-lipped throngs.

The Louisiana Weekly #4

DAVID HENDERSON

a phone duet over the radio
the night
we got our leading lady out of jail
they were talkin about handling niggers
the white folks was
one suggestion:
        in event of a riot
          to flood the canals in the negro section/
they probably got the idea
from the last flood/
when the big department stores were threatened
when they had to blow the industrial canal
                 to siphon some water off
happened to be right near black town the bombs fell
many blacks drowned
others were ferried by private boats
            for a fee
many blacks drowned
      the city
      never did get
      all the names

right on: white america

SONIA SANCHEZ

this country might have
been a pio
            neer land
once.
    but.   there ain't
no mo
        indians   blowing
custer's mind
            with a different
image of america.
                    this country
might have
            needed shoot/
outs/ daily/
        once.
                but. there ain't
no mo real/ white/   allamerican
                        bad/guys.
just.
    u & me.
            blk/ and un/armed.
this country might have
been a pion
        eer land.   once.
                    and it still is.
check out
        the falling
gun/shells   on our blk/tomorrows.

Rhythm Is a Groove (#2)

LARRY NEAL

Rhythm is a groove/packed against sweat flesh/
an afternoon in Mt. Morris Park.

The colored sun against black skin/bands moist/
/the heat/
/hands hot/the skins speak.

colored sun'gainst the beat
the beat against black motion
to flame and dance
while packed into the beat.

the park becomes Africa:
all clap hands and sing
ALL CLAP HANDS AND SING
do the foot shuffle/the color/
shuffle the beat, and the skins speak.

Sun come black, ju-ju wonder song.
Sun come black, ju-ju wonder song.
drum sing, speak black, black skin skin
shuffle the beat, shuffle the color/the beat speaks/
color the shuffle/black brother brother/
brother, brother, hurl drum into sky
make sun come, hot pulse flaming. YEAH!!!

Now, All You Children
RAY DUREM

Now, all you children of the night
gather round, Hey!
From ebony to almost white,
stop and listen . . . Bebop!
I'll explain where Justice hides,
why the black man walks and the Paddy rides,
and why the white man never lies!
Bebop!

I'm hip to all the rules.
Why little black children need cheaper schools
and can't use no swimmin' pools!
Bebop!
Why white women curl their hair,
and lay out in the sun, all bare,
tryin' to look like the Sister there,
Hey now!

Incident

COUNTEE CULLEN

Once riding in old Baltimore,
    Heart-filled, head-filled with glee,
I saw a Baltimorean
    Keep looking straight at me.

Now I was eight and very small,
    And he was no whit bigger,
And so I smiled, but he poked out
    His tongue, and called me, "Nigger."

I saw the whole of Baltimore
    From May until December;
Of all the things that happened there
    That's all that I remember.

From *Riot Rimes: USA*

RAYMOND R. PATTERSON

2

I felt this itching all over
My skin
So I smashed that plate-glass window in,
And all that fancy furniture
And easy credit plans
Were right there in my hands—
All the things that I've been needing.
And I didn't know my hands were bleeding.

3

The cop said I threw a brick
Then he took this great big stick
And hit me six times quick.
But I didn't, but I might
If my poor head ever gets right.

26

When it was ended
And we looked for some meaning
Among the dead
It seemed that Death himself
Had come
And rioted.

From *26 Ways of Looking at a Blackman*

RAYMOND R PATTERSON

There is the sorrow of blackmen
Lost in cities. But who can conceive
of cities lost in a blackman?

Riot Laugh & I Talk
DAVID HENDERSON

supermarket burning bomb
women who belong to no man
in pyres of burning flesh
machine gun bullets thru six-floor windows
picture window televisions coming in for the kill
vomiting fine snakes and dead babies
nuns land in flying saucers
red crosses on top

I Substitute for the Dead Lecturer
LEROI JONES

> *What is most precious, because*
> *it is lost. What is lost,*
> *because it is most*
> *precious.*

They have turned, and say that I am dying.
That
I have thrown
my life
away. They
have left me alone, where
there is no one, nothing
save who I am. Not a note
nor a word.

      Cold air batters
the poor (and their minds
turn open
like sores). What kindness
What wealth
can I offer? Except
what is, for me,
ugliest. What is
for me, shadows, shrieking
phantoms. Except
they have need
of life. Flesh

at least,
       should be theirs.

The Lord has saved me
to do this. The Lord
has made me strong. I
am as I must have
myself. Against all
thought, all music, all
my soft loves.

      For all these wan roads
I am pushed to follow, are
my own conceit. A simple muttering
elegance, slipped in my head
pressed on my soul, is my heart's
worth. And I am frightened
that the flame of my sickness
will burn off my face. And leave
the bones, my stewed black skull,
an empty cage of failure.

I Have Seen Black Hands
RICHARD WRIGHT

I

I am black and I have seen black hands, millions and millions of
  them—
Out of millions of bundles of wool and flannel tiny black fingers have
  reached restlessly and hungrily for life.
Reached out for the black nipples at the black breasts of black moth-
  ers,
And they've held red, green, blue, yellow, orange, white, and purple
  toys in the childish grips of possession,
And chocolate drops, peppermint sticks, lollypops, wineballs, ice
  cream cones, and sugared cookies in fingers sticky and gummy,
And they've held balls and bats and gloves and marbles and jack-
  knives and sling-shots and spinning tops in the thrill of sport and
  play,
And pennies and nickels and dimes and quarters and sometimes on
  New Year's, Easter, Lincoln's Birthday, May Day, a brand new
  green dollar bill,
They've held pens and rulers and maps and tablets and books in
  palms spotted and smeared with ink,
And they've held dice and cards and half-pint flasks and cue sticks
  and cigars and cigarettes in the pride of new maturity . . .

II

I am black and I have seen black hands, millions and millions of
  them—
They were tired and awkward and calloused and grimy and covered
  with hangnails,
And they were caught in the fast-moving belts of machines and
  snagged and smashed and crushed,

And they jerked up and down at the throbbing machines massing
taller and taller the heaps of gold in the banks of bosses,
And they piled higher and higher the steel, iron, the lumber, wheat,
rye, the oats, corn, the cotton, the wool, the oil, the coal, the meat,
the fruit, the glass, and the stone until there was too much to be
used,
And they grabbed guns and slung them on their shoulders and
marched and groped in trenches and fought and killed and con-
quered nations who were customers for the goods black hands had
made.
And again black hands stacked goods higher and higher until there
was too much to be used,
And then the black hands held trembling at the factory gates the
dreaded lay-off slip,
And the black hands hung idle and swung empty and grew soft and
got weak and bony from unemployment and starvation,
And they grew nervous and sweaty, and opened and shut in anguish
and doubt and hesitation and irresolution . . .

III

I am black and I have seen black hands, millions and millions of
them—
Reaching hesitantly out of days of slow death for the goods they had
made, but the bosses warned that the goods were private and did
not belong to them,
And the black hands struck desperately out in defence of life and there
was blood, but the enraged bosses decreed that this too was wrong,
And the black hands felt the cold steel bars of the prison they had
made, in despair tested their strength and found that they could
neither bend nor break them,

And the black hands fought and scratched and held back but a thou-
    sand white hands took them and tied them,
And the black hands lifted palms in mute and futile supplication to
    the sodden faces of mobs wild in the revelries of sadism,
And the black hands strained and clawed and struggled in vain at the
    noose that tightened about the black throat,
And the black hands waved and beat fearfully at the tall flames that
    cooked and charred the black flesh . . .

IV

    I am black and I have seen black hands
    Raised in fists of revolt, side by side with the white fists of white work-
        ers,
    And some day—and it is only this which sustains me—
    Some day there shall be millions and millions of them,
    On some red day in a burst of fists on a new horizon!

In Memoriam:
Rev. Martin Luther King, Jr. (Part One)

JUNE JORDAN

honey people murder mercy U.S.A.
the milkland turn to monsters teach
to kill to violate pull down destroy
the weakly freedom growing fruit
from being born

America

tomorrow yesterday rip rape
exacerbate despoil disfigure
crazy running threat the
deadly thrall
appall belief dispel
the wildlife burn the breast
the onward tongue
the outward hand
deform the normal
rainy riot sunshine
shelter wreck of darkness
derogate delimit blank
explode deprive
assassinate and batten up
like bullets fatten up
the raving greed
reactivate a springtime

terrorizing
duplication death
by death by men by more
than you or I can
STOP

ATTITUDES OF SOUL

*

*Soul is the ready spirit that
supports the person, that protects
the promise that, together with
the daily doing, styles a life
particular, real, and fully loving.*

*Let these last poems sure commune
our impulse to the hourly
flourishing of our soul.*

Motto

LANGSTON HUGHES

I play it cool
And dig all jive.
That's the reason
I stay alive.

My motto,
As I live and learn,
   is:
Dig And Be Dug
In Return.

The White House

CLAUDE MCKAY

Your door is shut against my tightened face,
And I am sharp as steel with discontent;
But I possess the courage and the grace
To bear my anger proudly and unbent.
The pavement slabs burn loose beneath my feet,
A chafing savage, down the decent street;
And passion rends my vitals as I pass,
Where boldly shines your shuttered door of glass.
Oh, I must search for wisdom every hour,
Deep in my wrathful bosom sore and raw,
And find in it the superhuman power
To hold me to the letter of your law!
Oh, I must keep my heart inviolate
Against the potent poison of your hate.

O Daedalus, Fly Away Home

ROBERT HAYDEN

Drifting night in the Georgia pines,
coonskin drum and jubilee banjo.
  Pretty Malinda, dance with me.

Night is juba, night is conjo.
  Pretty Malinda, dance with me.

Night is an African juju man
weaving a wish and a weariness together
  to make two wings.

  O fly away home fly away

Do you remember Africa?

  O cleave the air fly away home

My gran, he flew back to Africa,
just spread his arms and
  flew away home.

Drifting night in the windy pines;
night is a laughing, night is a longing.
  Pretty Malinda, come to me.

Night is a mourning juju man
weaving a wish and a weariness together
  to make two wings.

O fly away home fly away

November Cotton Flower

JEAN TOOMER

Boll-weevil's coming, and the winter's cold,
Made cotton-stalks look rusty, seasons old,
And cotton, scarce as any southern snow,
Was vanishing; the branch, so pinched and slow,
Failed in its function as the autumn rake;
Drouth fighting soil had caused the soil to take
All water from the streams; dead birds were found
In wells a hundred feet below the ground—
Such was the season when the flower bloomed.
Old folks were startled, and it soon assumed
Significance. Superstition saw
Something it had never seen before:
Brown eyes that loved without a trace of fear,
Beauty so sudden for that time of year.

I Know I'm Not Sufficiently Obscure

RAY DUREM

I know I'm not sufficiently obscure
to please the critics—nor devious enough.
Imagery escapes me.
I cannot find those mild and gracious words
to clothe the carnage.
Blood is blood and murder's murder.
What's a lavender word for lynch?
Come, you pale poets, wan, refined and dreamy:
here is a black woman working out her guts
in a white man's kitchen
for little money and no glory.
How should I tell that story?
There is a black boy, blacker still from death,
face down in the cold Korean mud.
Come on with your effervescent jive
explain to him why he ain't alive.
Reword our specific discontent
into some plaintive melody,
a little whine, a little whimper,
not too much—and no rebellion!
God, no! Rebellion's much too corny.
You deal with finer feelings,
very subtle—an autumn leaf
hanging from a tree—I see a body!

Sorrow Is the Only Faithful One

OWEN DODSON

Sorrow is the only faithful one:
The lone companion clinging like a season
To its original skin no matter what the variations.

If all the mountains paraded
Eating the valleys as they went
And the sun were a cliffure on the highest peak,

Sorrow would be there between
The sparkling and the giant laughter
Of the enemy when the clouds come down to swim.

But I am less, unmagic, black,
Sorrow clings to me more than to doomsday mountains
Or erosion scars on a palisade.

Sorrow has a song like a leech
Crying because the sand's blood is dry
And the stars reflected in the lake

Are water for all their twinkling
And bloodless for all their charm.
I have blood, and a song.
SORROW IS THE ONLY FAITHFUL ONE.

An Agony. As Now.
LEROI JONES

I am inside someone
who hates me. I look
out from his eyes. Smell
what fouled tunes come in
to his breath. Love his
wretched women.

Slits in the metal, for sun. Where
my eyes sit turning, at the cool air
the glance of light, or hard flesh
rubbed against me, a woman, a man,
without shadow, or voice, or meaning.

This is the enclosure (flesh,
where innocence is a weapon. An
abstraction. Touch. (Not mine.
Or yours, if you are the soul I had
and abandoned when I was blind and had
my enemies carry me as a dead man
(if he is beautiful, or pitied.

It can be pain. (As now, as all lies
flesh hurts me.) It can be that. Or
pain. As when she ran from me into
that forest.

        Or pain, the mind
silver spiraled whirled against the
sun, higher than even old men thought

God would be. Or pain. And the other. The
yes. (Inside his books, his fingers. They
were withered yellow flowers and were never
beautiful.) The yes. You will, lost soul, say
'beauty.' Beauty, practiced, as the tree. The
slow river. A white sun in its wet sentences.
Or, the cold men in their gale. Ecstasy. Flesh
or soul. The yes. (Their robes blown. Their bowls
empty. They chant at my heels, not at yours.) Flesh
or soul, as corrupt. Where the answer moves too quickly.
Where the God is a self, after all.)

Cold air blown through narrow blind eyes. Flesh,
white hot metal. Glows as the day with its sun.
It is a human love, I live inside. A bony skeleton
you recognize as words or simple feeling.

But it has no feeling. As the metal, is hot, it is not,
given to love.

It burns the thing
inside it. And that thing
screams.

Midway

NAOMI LONG MADGETT

I've come this far to freedom
And I won't turn back.
I'm climbing to the highway
From my old dirt track.

I'm coming and I'm going
And I'm stretching and I'm growing
And I'll reap what I've been sowing
Or my skin's not black.

I've prayed and slaved and waited
And I've sung my song.
You've bled me and you've starved me
But I've still grown strong.

You've lashed me and you've treed me
And you've everything but freed me
But in time you'll know you need me
And it won't be long.

I've seen the daylight breaking
High above the bough.
I've found my destination and I've made my vow;
So whether you abhor me
Or deride me or ignore me,
Mighty mountains loom before me
And I won't stop now.

One Thousand Nine Hundred & Sixty-Eight Winters

JACI EARLEY

Got up this morning
Feeling good & black
Thinking black thoughts
Did black things
Played all my black records
And minded my own black business
Put on my best black clothes
Walked out my black door
And, Lord have mercy: white snow!

Yet Do I Marvel
COUNTEE CULLEN

I doubt not God is good, well-meaning, kind,
And did He stoop to quibble could tell why
The little buried mole continues blind,
Why flesh that mirrors Him must someday die,
Make plain the reason tortured Tantalus
Is baited by the fickle fruit, declare
If merely brute caprice dooms Sisyphus
To struggle up a never-ending stair.
Inscrutable His ways are, and immune
To catechism by a mind too strewn
With petty cares to slightly understand
What awful brain compels His awful hand
Yet do I marvel at this curious thing:
To make a poet black, and bid him sing!

Dream Variation

LANGSTON HUGHES

To fling my arms wide
In some place of the sun,
To whirl and to dance
Till the white day is done.
Then rest at cool evening
Beneath a tall tree
While night comes on gently,
     Dark like me—
That is my dream!

To fling my arms wide
In the face of the sun,
Dance! Whirl! Whirl!
Till the quick day is done.
Rest at pale evening . . .
A tall, slim tree . . .
Night coming tenderly
     Black like me.

We Have Been Believers
MARGARET WALKER

We have been believers believing in the black gods of an old land, be-
lieving in the secrets of the seeress and the magic of the charmers
and the power of the devil's evil ones.

And in the white gods of a new land we have been believers believing
in the mercy of our masters and the beauty of our brothers, believ-
ing in the conjure of the humble and the faithful and the pure.

Neither the slavers' whip nor the lynchers' rope nor the bayonet could
kill our black belief. In our hunger we beheld the welcome table and
in our nakedness the glory of a long white robe. We have been be-
lievers in the new Jerusalem.

We have been believers feeding greedy grinning gods, like a Moloch
demanding our sons and our daughters, our strength and our wills
and our spirits of pain. We have been believers, silent and stolid and
stubborn and strong.

We have been believers yielding substance for the world. With our
hands have we fed a people and out of our strength have they wrung
and necessities of a nation. Our song has filled the twilight and our
hope has heralded the dawn.

Now we stand ready for the touch of one fiery iron, for the cleansing
breath of many molten truths, that the eyes of the blind may see
and the ears of the deaf may hear and the tongues of the people be
filled with living fire.

Where are our gods that they leave us asleep? Surely the priests and the preachers and the powers will hear. Surely now that our hands are empty and our hearts too full to pray they will understand. Surely the sires of the people will send us a sign.

We have been believers believing in our burdens and our demigods too long. Now the needy no longer weep and pray; the long-suffering arise, and our fists bleed against the bars with a strange insistency.

Nocturne Varial
LEWIS ALEXANDER

"I came as a shadow,
I stand now a light;
The depth of my darkness
Transfigures your night.

My soul is a nocturne
Each note is a star;
The light will not blind you
So look where you are.

The radiance is soothing.
There's warmth in the light.
I came as a shadow,
To dazzle your night!"

From the Dark Tower

COUNTEE CULLEN

We shall not always plant while others reap
The golden increment of bursting fruit,
Not always countenance, abject and mute,
That lesser men should hold their brothers cheap;
Not everlastingly while others sleep
Shall we beguile their limbs with mellow flute,
Not always bend to some more subtle brute;
We were not made eternally to weep.

The night whose sable breast relieves the stark,
White stars is no less lovely being dark,
And there are buds that cannot bloom at all
In light, but crumble, piteous, and fall;
So in the dark we hide the heart that bleeds,
And wait, and tend our agonizing seeds.

We Wear the Mask

PAUL LAURENCE DUNBAR

We wear the mask that grins and lies,
It hides our cheeks and shades our eyes,–
This debt we pay to human guile;
With torn and bleeding hearts we smile,
And mouth with myriad subtleties.

Why should the world be overwise,
In counting all our tears and sighs?
Nay, let them only see us, while
    We wear the mask.

We smile, but O great Christ, our cries
To Thee from tortured souls arise.
We sing, but oh, the clay is vile
Beneath our feet, and long the mile;
But let the world dream otherwise,
    We wear the mask.

If We Must Die

CLAUDE MCKAY

If we must die—let it not be like hogs
Hunted and penned in an inglorious spot,
While round us bark the mad and hungry dogs,
Making their mock at our accursed lot.
If we must die—oh, let us nobly die,
So that our precious blood may not be shed
In vain; then even the monsters we defy
Shall be constrained to honor us though dead!
Oh, Kinsmen! We must meet the common foe;
Though far outnumbered, let us show us brave,
And for their thousand blows deal one deathblow!
What though before us lies the open grave?
Like men we'll face the murderous, cowardly pack,
Pressed to the wall, dying, but fighting back!

Contributors

LEWIS ALEXANDER, born in 1900 in Washington, D.C., earned his degree at Howard University and then pursued further studies at the University of Pennsylvania. In addition to the appearance of his poems in anthologies and literary publications, a volume of his poetry has been published entitled *Enchantment*.

RUSSELL ATKINS was born in 1926 in Cleveland, Ohio. After studies at the Cleveland School of Art and the Cleveland Institute of Music, he pursued music theory into the development of "Psychovisualism." Members of the Cleveland Orchestra have performed some of his works, and his musical ideas have gained influential currency in Europe. His poetry has been published in numerous journals, including *Experiment, Botteghe Oscure, Podium,* and *Writers Forum*. His poems have been included in *Poetry of the Negro, American Negro Poetry,* and *Sixes and Sevens,* among other anthologies. His own volumes of poetry include *Phenomena, Two by Atkins, Objects,* and *Heretofore.* He died in 1978.

GWENDOLYN BROOKS, born 1917, moved early in her life from Topeka, Kansas, to Chicago, where she lived for much of her life. Graduating from Wilson Junior College in 1945, she went on to receive an American Academy of Arts and Letters award, a Guggenheim Fellowship, and the Pulitzer prize for poetry in 1949. Among her numerous books of published poems are *In the Mecca, A Street in Bronzeville, Annie Allen,* and *The Bean Eaters.* She died in 2003.

STERLING A. BROWN was born in Washington, D.C., in 1901. Having received degrees from Williams College and Harvard University, he taught English at Howard University. In 1937, he received a Guggenheim Fellowship. Published volumes of his poetry and criticism include *Southern Road, The Negro in American Fiction, Negro Poetry and Drama,* and *The Last Ride of Wild Bill.* He died in 1989.

KATHERINE L. CUESTAS (quoted during the first run of *soulscript*): "I was born on July 19, 1944, and had a most pleasant childhood as the youngest of four children. At thirteen I was hit by spinal meningitis, which reinforced and further developed a serious strain in my personality. As I look back I realize that my writing was a direct result of the loneliness that accompanied hospitalization and long convalescence." Miss Cuestas graduated from CCNY in 1966, and since then has taught elementary school children and worked for the New York City Youth Board and the Department of Social Services. Her poetry has appeared in the anthology *Beyond the Blues* and in *Ik Ben de Nieuwe Neger.* She says, "I continue to write because of the personal need that it fulfills. Unfortunately my poems know no color and one cannot tell that they are written by a Negro. Therefore, publishers looking for 'black poetry' are not interested in my works."

COUNTEE CULLEN was born in 1903. He earned his master's degree at Harvard University and went on to teach in New York City. *Color*, his first volume of poetry, received the Harmon Gold Award. Widely published during his lifetime, and afterward in anthologies, his books include *On These I Stand*, *The Black Christ*, and *The Lost Zoo*. He died in 1946.

LINDA CURRY was born, 1953, in Harlem. Her poetry has been published in *UHURU*, *The Teachers College Record*, and *Here I Am* (anthology), and she was the editor of the literary magazine *The Voice of the Children*.

DJANGATOLUM (Lloyd M. Corbin, Jr.) was born in 1949. After attending New York City public schools, he entered the Upward Bound Program at Brandeis University. He writes (during the first run of *soulscript*): "I have lived in Harlem-Bedford Stuyvesant-Harlem-Bedford Stuyvesant-Crown Heights-Harlem sections of New York in that order. My poems have appeared in *The Writers Workshop Anthology*, *What's Happening Magazine*, *CAW* (Students for a Democratic Society), *Look* magazine, and *The Me Nobody Knows*."

OWEN DODSON was born, 1914, in Brooklyn, New York. He earned degrees from Bates College and from Yale University, where two of his plays were produced. His poems have appeared in several anthologies including *I Am the Darker Brother* and *American Negro Poetry*. The first volume of his poetry is entitled *Powerful Long Ladder*. He died in 1983.

ALFRED DUCKETT (quoted during the first run of *soulscript*): "I am very pleased that you want to use my sonnet. I think a biography of the poem itself could be more important than a biography of me. It was written during World War II and the late Langston Hughes called it 'one of the best poems to come out of World War II.' It has been reprinted a number of times, meaning that it has a relevance to the situation of our fighting men today."

PAUL LAURENCE DUNBAR, the son of former slaves, was born in Dayton, Ohio, in 1872. He was employed as an elevator operator when his first book of poetry, *Oak and Ivy* (1893), appeared. His other volumes of poetry were *Majors and Minors, Lyrics of a Lowly Life, Lyrics of Love and Laughter*, and *Lyrics of Sunshine and Shadow*. He died in 1906.

RAY DUREM was born in 1915 in Seattle, Washington. His poems have been published in *Negro Digest* and in *Umbra*. His poetry appears in several anthologies, including *I Am the Darker Brother*. In 1963, he died in Los Angeles, California, after living for some time in Mexico.

JACQUELYN (JACI) EARLEY writes that she was born to this slave name during the twentieth century. She spent her growing years in Cambridge, Ohio, guided by her parents, Herbert and Lillian Earley. She describes her education as "some grade school, some high school, and some college." Her poems have been published in *Liberator, Revolt, Journal of Black Poetry*, and *Black Culture Weekly*. She indicates that her "general involvement" is survival, and that her "specific involvement" is revolution through change.

NIKKI GIOVANNI was born in Knoxville, Tennessee, in 1943. She attended Fisk University, where she majored in history and graduated in 1967. Her volumes of poetry include *Black Judgment; Black Feeling, Black Talk; Quilting the Black-Eyed Pea: Poems and Not-Quite Poems;* and *Love Poems*. Her individual poems have appeared in numerous journals, including *Negro Digest, Black Dialogue*, and *The Journal of Black Poetry*. Her work appears in a number of anthologies, including *New Black Poetry, Black Poetry, Black Art*, and *City in All Directions*.

MICHAEL GOODE (quoted during the first run of *Soulscript*): "I was born in Brooklyn Hospital, December 27, 1954. I have been published in *The Village Voice, The Teachers College Record*, and *The Now Voices*."

ROBERT HAYDEN was born in Detroit, Michigan in 1913. With the poet Myron O'Higgins, he published *The Lion and the Archer*. His individual poems have been printed in numerous magazines, including *The Atlantic Monthly*, *Negro Digest*, and *Poetry*. He is the author of several volumes of poetry, including *Heart-Shape in the Dust* (1940) and *Selected Poems* (1966). He is represented in many anthologies, *American Negro Poetry* among them. He received the Hopwood Award for Poetry, and fellowships and grants from the Rosenwald Foundation, the Carnegie Foundation, and The Fund for the Advancement of Education. At the International Festival of Negro Arts, at Dakar, Senegal, in 1966, he won first prize for his *A Ballad of Remembrance*. He died in 1980. His *Collected Poems* was published in 1989.

DAVID HENDERSON's volumes of poetry include *Felix and the Silent Forest* and *De Mayor of Harlem*. His poetry appears in several anthologies, including *Black Fire* and *The New Black Poetry*, and has been published in *Negro Digest*, *Liberator*, *Kulchur*, *Freedomways*, and *Umbra*. He has been a participating writer in the Teachers and Writers Collaborative program and served as a Writer-in-Residence at City College, of the City University of New York.

CALVIN HERNTON was born in Chattanooga, Tennessee, in 1932. He studied at Talladega College and Fisk University. He has worked as an English teacher and has served as editor of *Umbra* magazine. He is the author of *Sex and Racism* (volume of essays), *Scarecrow*, *Medicine Man*, *White Papers for White Americans*, and *The Sexual Mountain and Black Women Writers: Adventures in Sex, Literature, and Real Life*. His first volume of poetry is entitled *The Coming of Chronos to the House of Nightsong*. He died in 2001.

M. CARL HOLMAN, a graduate of Lincoln University, the University of Chicago, and Yale, began his employment career as a machine operator. From 1966 to 1968, he served as Deputy Staff Director of the U.S. Commission on Civil Rights. He then acted as vice-president for policy and program development in the Urban Coalition. He has received a playwrighting award from Yale University, and a John Hay Whitney Fellowship in creative writing. His poems have appeared in several literary periodicals, and he is represented in *Poetry of the Negro*, an anthology edited by Arna Bontemps and Langston Hughes.

VANESSA HOWARD was born in Brooklyn in 1955. She attended Rothschild Junior High School, where she was an honor student, during *soulscript*'s first run. Her poetry has been published in *The Teachers and Writers Newsletter* and in the anthology *Here I Am*. Her poems appeared regularly in *The Voice of the Children* and in school literary magazines.

LANGSTON HUGHES, surely the African American poet best known to the world, was born in Missouri, 1902. He graduated from Lincoln University and thereafter pursued an extremely productive writing career centered on poetry. Novelist, playwright, and newspaper columnist, he was also the author of many children's books. He published two autobiographies, *The Big Sea* and *I Wonder As I Wander*. Among the eleven volumes of his poetry that have been published, *The Weary Blues*, *Ask Your Mama*, and *Shakespeare in Harlem* are a few titles. Consistently concerned with helping other black writers and poets into the public ear and mind, he was the editor of eight anthologies presenting Afro-American literature. In 1967, he died in Harlem, U.S.A., his home.

JAMES WELDON JOHNSON: Born in Jacksonville, Florida, he successfully pursued careers, among them: public school principal, lawyer, diplomat, and Executive Secretary of the N.A.A.C.P. While he was Professor of Creative Literature at Fisk University, he and his brother composed what has become to be regarded as the Negro National Anthem, "Lift Every Voice and Sing." Author of many lyrics for musicals and hit songs, several volumes of his poetry were published during his life: *Fifty Years and Other Poems*, *God's Trombones*, and *St. Peter Relates an Incident of the Resurrection Day.* He also edited the *Book of American Negro Poetry.* He died in 1938.

GAYL JONES was born in Lexington, Kentucky, November 23, 1949. There she attended elementary and high school. Miss Jones' *Night of the Leopard,* a theater poem, has been published in *Silo,* 1969. She has gone on to author the novels *Corregidora, Eva's Man,* and *The Healing.*

LEROI JONES (now known as Amiri Baraka): Born in Newark, New Jersey, 1934, he studied at Howard and Columbia universities. Poet, short-story writer, dramatist, social analyst, his poetry has appeared in countless anthologies that present the contemporary poem and black poetry. His volumes of poetry include *Preface to a Twenty Volume Suicide Note* and *The Dead Lecturer.* Individual essays of his have appeared in *Evergreen Review, Kulchur, Liberator, Midstream, The Nation,* and *Saturday Review,* among other magazines. He is the author of *Home,* a collection of his essays; *Tales,* a collection of his short stories; *Blues People,* a history of jazz; and *The System of Dante's Hell,* a novel. *Dutchman* and *The Slaveship* are among his best-known plays. He is coeditor of the anthology *Black Fire.*

JUNE JORDAN was born, 1936, in Harlem. As a journalist, she published essays and articles in *Esquire, Mademoiselle, The Nation, The Village Voice, Evergreen Review, The New York Times, The Urban Review,* and *Partisan Review.* She served as co-director of a creative writing workshop for black and Puerto Rican children in Brooklyn. Sponsored by the Academy of American Poets, she has read her poetry throughout the public schools of the city, and elsewhere. Individual poems have appeared in *Liberator, American Dialog, Negro Digest,* and in the anthologies *The New Black Poetry* and *In the Time of Revolution.* Her volumes of poetry include *Who Look At Me, some changes, haruko/love poems,* and *Kissing God Goodbye: Poems 1991–1997.* She received a Rockefeller Foundation grant in creative writing, and taught at Sarah Lawrence College, the City College of New York, and the University of California, Berkeley. She died in 2002.

BOB KAUFMAN was a black Beat poet whose published volumes of poetry include *Solitudes Crowded with Loneliness* and *Golden Sardine*. His work has been published in numerous journals of poetry. He died in 1986.

STEPHEN KWARTLER (quoted during the first run of *soulscript*): "I've been told I was born on January 31, 1950, in the Bronx. Having completed High School I am now employed by the New York Telephone Company. My plans are to continue writing and hope someone will want my type of poetry for publication. I haven't tried to publish any of my 'free style poetry' but hope to someday. If you or anyone are interested in my other poetry I will be most happy to cooperate. Right now I am involved in serious thinking in how to avoid the draft."

DON L. LEE was born in Little Rock, Arkansas, 1942. He attended high school, and graduated from junior college, in Chicago. His individual poems have appeared in *Negro Digest*, *Ebony* magazine, *The Journal of Black Poetry*, *Black Culture Weekly*, and several other black literary journals. His volumes of poetry include *Think Black*, *Black Pride*, and *Don't Cry, Scream*.

JULIUS LESTER was born, 1939, in Saint Louis, Missouri. Field Secretary for SNCC, the Student Non-violent Coordinating Committee, he was a regular columnist for *The Guardian* and conducted his own weekly radio program on WBAI, in New York. A folk singer of national renown, two albums of his singing, and his songs, have been released. He is the author of *Look Out, Whitey! black power's gon' get your mama!*, *To Be A Slave*, *Revolutionary Notes*, *Search for the New Land*, and *The Blues Singers: Ten Who Rocked the World*, among other titles, including many children's books.

AUDRE LORDE (quoted during the first run of *soulscript*): "I am black, woman poet. All three are outside of the realm of choice. I was born in New York. Last spring, under a National Endowment for the Arts grant, I spent some time as poet-in-residence at Tougaloo College in Jackson, Mississippi, where I became convinced, anti-academic though I am, that all poets must teach what they know, in order to continue being. I teach creative writing at City College, and a course in the Black Experience, at Lehman College. Neither replaces writing or being black. My first book, *The First Cities*, was printed in 1968; another will be coming at the end of 1969. I read wherever I think I can be heard, and have poems in Major's *New Black Poetry*, Hughes' *New Negro Poets, U.S.A.*, Poole's *Beyond the Blues*, and Brehman's *Sixes and Sevens*. My poetry has also appeared in *The Journal of Black Poetry*, *Negro Digest*, *Parasite*, and *Pound*." She died in 1992.

NAOMI LONG MADGETT was born in Norfolk, Virginia, and received an M.A. from Wayne University. Her poetry has been published in anthologies, and her volumes of poems include: *Songs to A Phantom Nightingale*, *The One and The Many*, and *Octavia: Guthrie and Beyond*.

CLARENCE MAJOR attended the Art Institute of Chicago and the University of Wisconsin. He is the editor of the anthology *The New Black Poetry*, and his poems have appeared in *Where is Vietnam?*, *Which Side Are You On?*, *American Negro Poetry*, plus other anthologies. He is a prolific author, and his books include *Swallow the Lake*, *Symptoms and Madness*, *Fun and Games*, *Dirty Bird Blues: A Novel*, and *Waiting for Sweet Betty*. His poems have also been published in numerous journals and magazines, including *Negro Digest*, *Literary Review*, *Umbra*, *Motive*, etc. He has directed the Harlem's Writers Workshop and has taught creative writing in the Teachers and Writers Collaborative program. Mr. Major has been sponsored by the Academy of American Poets in poetry readings and workshops. He has read his poetry at the Guggenheim Museum, the New School for Social Research, and at the Judson Church and Saint Marks-in-the-Bouwerie.

CLAUDE MCKAY: Born, 1889, in Jamaica, B.W.I., he arrived in the U.S.A., 1912, and spent two years studying agriculture at Kansas State University. He visited the Soviet Union in 1921. Associate editor of *The Liberator* and *The Masses*, he contributed to many current periodicals of his day. He is the author of *A Long Way from Home*, *Harlem Shadows*, and *Songs of Jamaica*, among other books. He died in 1948 in Chicago.

LARRY NEAL was born, 1937, in Atlanta, Georgia. He studied at Lincoln University and there received his B.A. Co-editor, with Amiri Baraka, of *Black Fire*, the anthology of African American prose, poetry, drama, and short stories, he also acted as editor of *Liberator*, *The Cricket*, and *Journal of Black Poetry*. His poetry has appeared in the anthology *For Malcolm*, in *Black Fire*, and in numerous journals of black literature. He died in 1981.

RAYMOND R. PATTERSON (quoted during first run of *soulscript*): "I was born December 14, 1929, in New York City. After public school on Long Island, I attended Lincoln University, Pennsylvania, and New York University, earning an M.A. degree in English. Since then, except for two years working in an institution for delinquent boys, I have been an English teacher. My poems have appeared in a number of anthologies including *New Negro Poets: U.S.A.*, *Poets of Today*, *For Malcolm*, and *New Black Poets*. *26 Ways of Looking at a Black Man and Other Poems* is my first volume of poetry, published by Award Books." He died in 2001.

ISHMAEL REED was born in 1938. His individual poems have appeared in *The Negro Digest* and *Liberator*. His articles and reviews have appeared in *The Writer*, *Arts Magazine*, and *The Los Angeles Free Press*. He is a co-founder of the *East Village Other*. He has published numerous novels, including *The Freelance Pallbearers* and *Yellow Back Radio Broke-Down*. He is currently living in California and is a professor at the University of California, Berkeley.

SONIA SANCHEZ was born in Alabama and attended Hunter College in New York. Her poems have been published in *Negro Digest* and *The Journal of Black Poetry*, and in the anthologies *Black Fire* and *The New Black Poetry*. Her own books include *Shake Loose My Skin* and *Like the Singing Coming Off the Drums: Love Poems*.

PHILLIP SOLOMON (quoted during first run of *soulscript*): "I was born in Brooklyn, in '54. As an educational background I went to Sands J.H.S., but am now attending Pine Point School in Connecticut, U.S.A. Now I am generally involved in writing two books. One is called *The Night Watchman* and the other is about race riots and black fighting to become *a part* of the Human race."

GLENN THOMPSON was born in Brooklyn, 1955, and attended Sands Junior High School. He wrote during *soulscript*'s first run that he is especially interested in science because "I am a very curious individual." His poetry appeared regularly in *The Voice of the Children*.

JEAN TOOMER was born in Washington, D.C., in 1893. Poet, playwright, and short-story writer, his novelette *Cane* returned to public celebrity and appreciation in 1969, after several decades of obscurity. *Cane*, a mingling of poetry and prose, represents innovative accomplishment of first magnitude. During his early career, his work was widely circulated, published, and respected. His poetry remains available in numerous anthologies, including *Poetry of the Negro, American Negro Poetry*, and *I Am the Darker Brother*. He died in 1967.

PAUL VESEY (Samuel Allen) was born in 1917 and is a graduate of Fisk University Law School. His volume of poetry *Ivory Tusks* was published in a bilingual edition in Germany in 1956. He was editor of a volume entitled *Pan-Africanism Reconsidered* and has translated Jean-Paul Sartre's *Black Orpheus* into English for the African literary magazine *Présence Africaine*. Mr. Allen has published numerous articles and essays on the African and Caribbean poets of *"négritude."* His poems appear in several anthologies.

MARGARET WALKER won the Yale University Younger Poets Prize in 1942 for her volume of poetry *For My People*. She received a Houghton Mifflin Literary Fellowship for her novel *Jubilee* in 1966. In 1997 the University of Tennessee Press published *On Being Female, Black and Free: Essays by Margaret Walker, 1932–1992*. She died in 1998.

JAY WRIGHT, born in 1935 in New Mexico, appears in the anthologies entitled *New Negro Poets, USA, Black Fire*, and others, and his work has been collected in the book *Transfigurations* (2000). He earned his B.A. from the University of California at Berkeley and an M.A. from Rutgers University, and received the Rockefeller Brothers Theological Fellowship.

RICHARD WRIGHT was born, 1908, in Natchez, Mississippi. His childhood is described in *Black Boy*, his powerful autobiography. He was mostly self-educated. *Uncle Tom's Children*, a collection of short stories, was his first book to be published. *Native Son*, his first novel, established his international reputation. Among his other books, there are *Twelve Million Black Voices, The Outsider, Black Power*, and *White Man, Listen!* His poetry appears in the anthologies *American Negro Poetry* and *I Am the Darker Brother*. For his last thirteen years, he lived as an expatriate in France. He died there in 1960.

Index of First Lines

Index of Authors

Permissions Acknowledgments

Thanks are due to the following for permission to include copyrighted selections:

Mrs. Anna Thompson for "Nocturne Varial" by Lewis Alexander.

Samuel Allen (Paul Vesey) for his "American Gothic," Copyright © 1963 by Samuel Allen.

Russell Atkins for his "It's Here In The."

Harper Brothers, Publishers, Inc., for "The Bean Eaters" and "The Ballad of Rudolph Reed," from *Selected Poems* by Gwendolyn Brooks.

Sterling A. Brown for his "After Winter."

Lloyd Corbin (Djangatolum) for his "Dedication to the Final Confrontation," Copyright © 1970 by Lloyd Corbin.

Katherine L. Cuestas for her "Poem."

Harper Brothers, Publishers, Inc., for "Fruit of the Flower," "Incident," "From the Dark Tower," and "Yet Do I Marvel," from *On These I Stand* by Countee Cullen.

Farrar, Straus & Giroux, Inc., for "Sorrow Is the Only Faithful One" and "Counterpoint" from *Powerful Long Ladder* by Owen Dodson, Copyright © 1946 by Owen Dodson.

Alfred A. Duckett for his "Sonnet,"

Dodd, Mead & Company, Inc., for "We Wear the Mask" from *The Complete Poems of Paul Laurence Dunbar.*

Dorothy Durem for "Now, All You Children," "I Know I'm Not Sufficiently Obscure," and "Award," by Ray Durem.

Jaci Earley for her "One Thousand Nine Hundred & Sixty-Eight Winters."

Nikki Giovanni and the Broadside Press for "NIKKI-ROSA" by Nikki Giovanni.

October House, Inc., for "O Daedalus, Fly Away Home," "Those Winter Sundays," "Frederick Douglass," and "Runagate Runagate," from *Selected Poems* by Robert Hayden, Copyright © 1966 by Robert Hayden.

David Henderson for his "Five winters age" and "Number 5—December," Copyright © 1967 by David Henderson, and "Riot Laugh & I Talk" and "The Louisiana Weekly #4," Copyright © 1968 by David Henderson.

Calvin C. Hernton for his "Madhouse" and "The Distant Drum," Copyright © 1970 by Calvin Hernton.

M. Carl Holman for his "Song," Copyright © 1970 by M. Carl Holman.

Alfred A. Knopf, Inc., for "Dream Variation," "My People," and "Mother to Son" from *Selected Poems* by Langston Hughes, Copyright © 1926 by Alfred A. Knopf, Inc., and renewed 1954 by Langston Hughes; "Motto" from *The Panther and the Lash* by Langston Hughes, Copyright © 1951 by Langston Hughes.

The Viking Press, Inc., for "The Creation" from *God's Trombones* by James Weldon Johnson, Copyright © 1927 by the Viking Press; renewed 1955 by Grace Nail Johnson.

Gayl Jones for her "Many Die Here," "tripart," and "Satori."

The Sterling Lord Agency for "As a possible lover," "I Substitute for the Dead Lecturer," "The end of man is his beauty," and "An Agony. As Now." by LeRoi Jones, Copyright © 1964 by LeRoi Jones.

Corinth Books for "Preface to a Twenty Volume Suicide Note" by LeRoi Jones.

New Directions Publishing Corporation for "To My Son Parker, Asleep in the Next Room" and "Blues Note," from *Solitudes Crowded with Loneliness*, Copyright © 1961, 1965 by Bob Kaufman.

Stephen Kwartler for his "Epilogue," Copyright © 1970 by Stephen Kwartler.

Don L. Lee and the Broadside Press for "A Poem Looking for a Reader" by Don L. Lee.

Ronald Hobbs Literary Agency and Julius Lester for his "On the Birth of My Son, Malcolm Coltrane," and "lxvxii," Copyright © 1970 by Julius Lester, "Mud in Vietnam," Copyright © 1967 by Julius Lester.

Printed in the United States
by Baker & Taylor Publisher Services